# The Profit Game

Published by
Capital Books Inc.
22883 Quicksilver Drive
Sterling, Virginia 20166

LIBRARY OF CONGRESS CATALOGING-IN-PUBLICATION DATA
Schimel, Barry R., 1941-
The profit game : how to play, how to win / Barry R. Schimel and Gary R. Kravitz.
p. cm.
Includes bibliographical references and index.
ISBN 1-892123-01-0
1. Small business–Finance. 2. Strategic planning.
3. Management. I. Kravitz, Gary R. II. Title.
HG4027.7.2355 1998 98-29091
658.15'92–dc21 CIP

**Attention Organizations:**

# The Profit Game

## How to Play—How to Win

By Barry R. Schimel, CPA

Gary R. Kravitz and

Mark W. Williams, CPA, PFS

CAPITAL BOOKS, INC.

Sterling, Virginia

# CHEERS!

For the evolution, production, and creativity of this book, we cheer our fans. They have made this undertaking possible:


• To our clients who continue to make it possible for us to improve their profit*ability*. You learn so much from us and we learn so much from you.

• To the Institute of Profit Advisors (U.S.) and the Association of Profit Advisors (U.K.) for their confidence in us. Thanks for letting us work with you, so that you will continue to make a positive difference for your clients.

• To Practice Development Institute, LLC (PDI), Allan D. Koltin, President; David Ross and their support team, for working with us to serve approximately 100 leading edge business consulting firms who proactively deliver our system to their clients. Thanks for your much-appreciated efforts.

• To the more than 100 trade associations who have given us the opportunity to share our message with their members by speaking at their conventions and publishing our articles in their magazines and newsletters.

• To our Capital Books publisher, Kathleen Hughes, for being our "Profit Game" coach. She helped us document the many thoughts, systems, and activities that characterize this book. Her patience, persistence, and creativity make an All-Star Coach.

• To all the families of our "Team," whose devotion and support make all the difference in the world. Without their patience, understanding, and great ideas, this book would not have been possible.

• To Elinor Schimel, Barry Schimel's wife, for all of her brainstorming, sharing of creative ideas and thoughts on how to make this book so meaningful to all readers. Also special thanks for all the times Barry drove her crazy with more new ideas involving his desire to help businesses improve their profitability, so many of which are described in this book.

• To Barry J. Friedman, long-time friend and wonderful team strategist—every successful team needs a master strategist.

• To "The Profit Game" team, Captain Barry R. Schimel applauds his coaches, co-authors Gary R. Kravitz and Mark W. Williams. This book has brought three dynamic yet different people together to create a winning team. And, to our assistant coaches, Dina H. Morrison and Chuck Cain, whose tireless implementation of our strategies made this project possible. Not only has the creation of this book been intellectually fulfilling, but also it has been one of our greatest professional experiences. We wouldn't be teammates if it were not for the Profit Game. Our team has learned how to play and how to win!

# The Profit Game

## How to Play—How to Win

Business is the game.
The objective is to score profits.

In sports, players understand the rules for playing the game, know what's expected of them as team members, are coached and practice their skills, know how to score. Plus every successful sports team has strategies for winning, and everyone on the team learns what those strategies are. Players strive to reach their potential. Team members strive to maximize the score. They like playing because competing is exciting and it is fun to win.

In business, although people go to work every day, do they understand the big picture, its rules, or how to improve the score? Are they coached to maximize their skills and understand their role as a team member? Do they know the score, or even if their team is winning or losing? Have the players and profits reached their potential?

This book is about playing the game of business—scoring profits for the benefit of everyone in the company. It teaches you to score, be a winner, and develop greater profit*ability*.

We dedicate this book to everyone who wants to make *The Profit Game* a game worth playing.

## THE PROFIT GAME
### How to Play—How to Win

## CONTENTS

# Introduction

## THE PROFIT OPTION

When we first open a dialogue with business leaders, it's amazing how many of them tell us: "I really don't think there is anything more we could do to increase profits. We're doing everything we can, I'm sure."

Yet we know that owners and managers live in constant fear of what tomorrow will bring. What if your new product is so successful you can't produce enough of them? What's going to happen next to knock you off your perch? What if you lose customers? What if the plant equipment fails? What if someone sues your socks off? What if in ten or fifteen years you want to sell your firm and get your money out of it, and you don't have anyone who can operate at the same level you do? If the company has to "downsize," where will you be? What assurance do you have of continued—or any—success?

Without a system for generating continued profits, the answer to the last and most important question is...none.

Fortunately, many business owners have been savvy enough to find out more about the Profit Enhancement Process and have been willing to let us help them discover and achieve their unrealized profit potential. It's these partnerships that have turned into our most gratifying testimonials. This one is from Gilbert Carpel, CEO of Washington Express:

"I must admit that my personal expectations were not very high since we have, for three years, been aggressively and continuously seeking ways to improve our bottom line. I was, therefore, quite surprised that we were able to identify an additional $500,000 per year in unrealized profits."

We all know that profit is the fuel that powers a business. Profit fuels growth, rewards your shareholders and stakeholders, and ultimately determines the success or failure of your enterprise. Profit is what gives a business opportunities, choices, and options. It's what provides funds for new acquisitions and for research and development of new products and services to add value to your business. It's what provides the cash for increasing salaries, bonuses and benefits; for training; for new technology and equipment; for reducing debt; for more effective marketing and promotion; and for enhancing working conditions. At the same time, it's what provides personal security. A company that is reaching for its profit potential is an exciting place to work. Everyone likes to be associated with a winner.

And when a company does reach its profit potential, everyone involved feels a sense of accomplishment, enhanced egos, heightened self-esteem, and a chance for personal gain. Owners get a greater return on their investment and reap the cash benefits from their financial risk-taking and hard work.

We all know it takes continued profits to build longevity into a business. Without a process for generating recurring profits, any business won't be around long. Even the healthiest firms go through difficult financial periods. Many fail. Forty-six percent of the companies that made the Fortune 500 in 1981 were gone from the list by 1991.

Employees at all levels share top management's fear. Tough economic times mean they could lose their jobs. They can't plan for the future. A company on shaky financial footing means everyone's focus becomes short-term survival rather than capturing long-term opportunities. We spend at least one third of our adult life working. This time can be enjoyable. But it takes sustainable profits.

Having established that a never-ending profit generating machine is imperative for your business's survival. Here's a question for you! Do you have a plan for a profit in place?

You've probably got a decent business plan. You certainly have a good marketing plan. You may even have a solid "exit plan." But, do you have an astute "profit maximizing plan"—a plan that locks in the extra money you should be making from your business?

How important is a Profit Plan? It's vital. In today's highly competitive environment, all companies are looking for ways to improve their processes and increase their profitability. That generally means taking a step back to make an honest appraisal of where you stand. That's why you need a Profit Plan. It's like the game plan for winning the Super Bowl. It's a plan that focuses everyone in the business on the bottom line—no matter what their job is. It's a plan for realizing the profit potential your business is capable of generating. In business, it's "The Plan" that assists you in winning the Profit Game.

In this book you're going to learn how to develop a realistic Profit Plan for your business and put it to work. You're going to discover how to...

- Provide a forum for generating exciting new profit ideas from your managers and employees all down the line;
- Put the best of these ideas into a Profit Plan the entire company is committed to;
- Put that "game plan" to work generating immediate and longer-term bottom-line results—all in harmony with your company's strategic goals and objectives;
- And, best of all, keep the profits rolling in—during good times and bad.

We're going to reveal to you the profit management system that has already produced enormous profit results for already profitable businesses—literally hundreds of them in more than 40 different industries so far, plus not-for-profit organizations. It's a system that has discovered hundreds of millions of dollars of previously unrealized profits for the companies that have implemented their Profit Plan, and it never stops generating new profit ideas that fuel their next level of business development. It's a system that delivers never-ending profits to those who manage it effectively.

We call this system the Profit Enhancement Process, PEP for short. And we liken it to the process that a great football team goes through to compete in and win the Super Bowl. We believe winning in the business world is just like winning on the football field. To win the Super Bowl, you need a great head coach—a motivator with a vision of what the entire team is capable of accomplishing. You need excellent, motivated assistant coaches who are experts in their areas and know the strengths and weaknesses of the competition and their players. You need an excellent team with a goal in sight, conditioned to produce maximum results and motivated to win. And you need a well-thought-out game plan everyone understands and is committed to.

Like the best coaches, you'll learn how to...

- Share responsibility for profitability with your management team (soon to be a Profit Team);
- Identify financial strategies which will increase sales, maximize profit margins, and control expenses;
- Establish measurable financial goals that will enhance profitability;
- Install a system of accountability and responsibility that produces positive financial performance;
- Implement practical and logical business strategies that will turn ideas into bottom-line results.

PEP is really quite simple as compared to other popular management systems like Reengineering and Total Quality Management. They can be likened to the movie, *Field of Dreams.* In that film the Kevin Costner character stands in the cornfield listening to the voice that says, "Build it and they will come." If you launch a complex organization-wide endeavor that touches many people and processes and gets them working in sync, profits *may* come. Unfortunately, many companies have discovered that this isn't necessarily so. Some businesses now believe that TQM stands for Too Quirky to Manage and have employed the Profit Enhancement Process because of its practicality and sustainable results.

Without a system to discover ideas that were previously unimaginable and that measure progress, profits may not come.

That's why PEP emphasizes and supports the implementation process with as much rigor as the initial gathering of ideas and building of teams to carry them out.

This book will also give you some proven ideas to start generating greater profitability in your business, even if you never implement our entire system. Enhanced profitability is exciting, exhilarating, euphoric and an endless journey. This book is not about cost-cutting. Your company is in business to generate profits, not to cut costs. That is what this book is about.

We are called The Profit Advisors, and we're so convinced that PEP works that we'll reimburse you for the cost of the "basic training" you'll receive in this book (its purchase price) —if, after reading it, you can't turn your new knowledge into new profits. And if, and when, you would like help taking your new Profit Plan to the next level, contact us or one of almost 100 leading edge members of The Institute of Profit Advisors in the United States, an organization we co-founded along with Practice Development Institute, LLC (PDI). Our system is also being utilized in the United Kingdom by their Association of Profit Advisors, of which Barry Schimel (co-author of this book) is an honorary member.

Start improving your profits right now, in harmony with your company's goals and objectives. This book will turn you into the head coach and your managers into the assistant coaches who will lead your team into the Super Profit Bowl and win, season after season. Let's start training.

# Chapter 1

# Profit Training For Coaches

> We, as entrepreneurs, are always miles ahead in our vision from the realities of the present. We tend to focus on growth at the expense of profit, knowing that it is only a matter of time before the profits come. What we tend to forget is that the company's culture will tend to generate more growth at the expense of profit.
>
> —Mark Salman, CEO of La Parisienne Bakery

One of our more seasoned clients is a wholesale bakery. For the past two years, CEO Mark Salman has committed his company to the Profit Enhancement Process (PEP) to ensure that he and his employees are focused on profits as the business grows. He knows how easy it is for an owner to focus on growth (more sales, a bigger plant, more customers, more employees, bigger budgets) at the expense of that all-important bottom line. This CEO agrees with the client who informed us that sales feed one's ego and profit feeds one's family. The right question is: Where is your focus?

---

In profit management, making short-term goals is as important as attaining long-term goals.

---

La Parisienne Bakery has completed two Profit Super Bowls, or profit management retreats. This is the stage of our profit management system during which the Chief Executive Officer, managers and department heads create their Profit Plan for the coming business season. During the initial profit planning session, the department heads and managers analyzed the cost-effectiveness of their production and delivery schedules among other issues partially identified by "Coach" Salman. They discovered that they were not maximizing sales from customers who sell breakfast bakery products because they were not focused on delivering bagels and breakfast rolls before the morning rush. A Profit Champion and Profit Team were assigned the task of revising the production and delivery times to meet the retail store's schedule. Delivery of bakery products by 6 a.m. brought the company increased customer satisfaction and sales. A simple operational change meant big profits.

Before the second Profit Super Bowl, Mark met with his managers to congratulate them. He posted a chart demonstrating the growth in profits from the previous year. He reviewed each manager's successful profit projects. Then with a flourish, he opened his briefcase and handed each of them a bonus—a "token" of his appreciation for their good work. Do you think those managers went into their second Profit Super Bowl with high enthusiasm that year? You bet.

One of the issues identified that year was the company's need to improve its sanitation and equipment maintenance efforts. A Profit Team member came up with the brilliant idea of creating an "Adopt a Bakery Area" program, similar to the "Adopt a Highway" campaign. The management team devised a plan in which employees would volunteer to be responsible for a section of the bakery or a piece of equipment. Employees were to keep their "adopted" areas or equipment safe and clean, and make sure that regular maintenance was performed. To recognize employees for their efforts, the company placed signs in the adopted areas similar to the "Adopt a Highway" program, announcing the employees' roles in keeping the bakery safe, clean and operational. The results were reduced equipment and repair costs, improved bakery-goods production, and reduced worker's compensation claims because there were fewer accidents.

We'll watch the scoreboard with Mark for this company's third winning "season." This bakery now knows how to make dough rise!

---

Half of the word "profit" is "pro." Is the profitability of your business PROfessionally managed?

---

Your employees are your most valued players. Hidden in their minds are ideas for adding hundreds of thousands of dollars—maybe even millions—to your company's bottom line. They deal with your customers and your vendors and your production processes every day. They know where the problems and the opportunities are, but they may not know how to communicate them to you. The vital skill all players must have to score profits for your business—their "profit*ability*"—is undeveloped.

Some people are born with "profit*ability*." It's like athletic ability. For them it's a natural talent that enables them to find profit wherever it's hidden. But most people, like most athletes, must be coached on playing for profit, and everyone needs training (and that means coaching and practice) before they can hone these skills.

Look at the word "profit." Divide it into two syllables. The "pro" stands for *professional*, a person who has as much experience in the business world as a star athlete does on the field. And "fit" takes training, stamina and commitment to maintain peak performance. So what is "profit*ability*"? It's the skill necessary to look objectively at your entire business or a single department, determine what more can be done to add value to the bottom line, and the *ability* to turn ideas into financial results.

If you are an entrepreneur, you probably have natural "profit*ability*" or you wouldn't be where you are today. How many of your managers have this ability? And how about your employees? We are convinced that every employee knows where there is real money to be made in the minutiae of everyday business activity. The receptionist may have one suggestion, so might Joe from accounting. The trouble is, no one ever asks them to share their profit-generating ideas. In fact, employees don't even realize it's their job to do so, and there is no forum for it to happen.

For whatever reason, a lot of companies have no mechanism to promote profit-generating ideas to senior management. Part of the problem is that most employees, while they care about the company's success, feel that they were hired to do a job, perform a function, and nothing else. They think that little will change for them whether profits go up or down. It's the job of the head coach to change their perception, to make each and every one into a Profit Enhancement Officer or PEO. Winning the Profit Super Bowl will mean super benefits for the entire team.

---

Playing for profit means a new way of analyzing your team's performance.

---

The CEO of a trash removal company tried the Profit Enhancement Process. This particular firm has a fleet of trucks, and services businesses and residences in the suburbs of a large metropolitan area. During the Profit Super Bowl, the group identified one of their largest expenses as landfill charges. While empty, all of their trucks were weighed to establish a base weight. Each truck was certified with its exact weight empty. After a pickup route was completed, the truck went to the landfill to deposit its load. It was driven onto a scale, and the weight of the empty truck was subtracted, leaving the weight of the trash that was assessed at the appropriate landfill.

At first glance, this sounds like a pretty routine transaction. No room for extra profit here. But in reality, $78,000 per year of profit waste was discovered by one of the managers. It seems like a small detail, but she discovered that when the truck was driven onto the scale and weighed, the 150 to 200 pound driver and helper were still sitting in it. The trash truck driver and helper didn't even think about it, and neither did their supervisor. But when you consider the number of truck loads per day times the number of days in a year, an insignificant weight becomes very meaningful. Then further, multiply that by the number of trucks in the entire fleet.

---

TIMES x TIMES x TIMES =
Endless Profit Opportunities

---

The Profit Team immediately decreed that the trash collectors must get off their truck while it's being weighed. Out goes the truck driver and helper and in comes an extra $78,000 a year to this company's bottom line—in perfect harmony with the company's strategic goals and objectives.

Admit it. You're really in business to make profits—no matter what you make or do. It's okay to use the "P" word—Profits!

During our years as Profit Advisors, we've been astounded at how many companies know how to produce their product or sell their service, but don't realize the importance of profits. It's always the means to the end in business. Without it, financial dreams will never materialize.

When we review the clients' business goals with them, it's often like pulling teeth to get the owner to admit that his primary goal is to make his business more profit*able* so that the organization and everyone in the company has more options and choices. His initial focus is usually on growth in new business. His management team may be frustrated because they have concentrated their efforts on sales, but the company's bottom line has not dramatically improved.

As we work with clients like this, their perspective of the company begins to change. When the owner, finally, after much deliberation, answers, "To make more profit so that we have greater opportunities, options, and choices," everyone seems relieved. It's almost as if profit is a dirty word that is rarely mentioned.

When the words, "I'm in business to make a profit," come out of a CEO's mouth, it's like "Eureka, we've got it!" Everyone on the management team becomes very excited. Their enthusiasm has been dulled for so long while the business wanders aimlessly. Now a bright, new vision appears. It is often the beginning of the solution that will improve a company's financial performance because now everyone will focus on what needs to be done to improve profit*ability*. They know that everyone is the beneficiary when the organization reaches its profit potential.

Develop your bottom-line vision. You must first see it to capture it.

Reflect on all the time you spend in meetings. How many have dealt exclusively with ideas to improve profits? Do any of your various manuals, i.e., operations, personnel, and so forth, even mention the word *profit*? Do you have a bottom-line vision, a profit management system that clearly focuses your business on how to attain its primary goal—profit, the fuel necessary to power your business?

We assure you that if your business does not have a profit management system in place, it is probably not a fun place to work. It's like going to a football game where there is no scoreboard. Imagine the effort to advance a football 100 yards and neither players nor fans know if their team is winning or losing. Boring!

Are profits everybody's job? They certainly are! Why should your business pay salaries to employees who don't feel responsible or even know that their job is improving the bottom line? Managerial positions are often established to oversee functional processes within organizations, but who is responsible for bottom-line results?

---

The most successful leaders are those whose people state, "We did it ourselves," when the work is completed.

---

A manufacturing business called us in. The owner was frustrated. He knew that his business had greater profit potential than was being realized. His instinct told him that the company's bottom line was under performing, but he didn't know how to get a commitment from his management team to focus on improving the company's bottom line. He did not know how to involve his management team in the process of profit improvement. We got him a front row seat at a Profit Super Bowl.

At that time the business had experienced a previous year's loss of $200,000. His management team was comprised of the owner and 15 departmental managers. This group had two members who were identified as potential problems. One manager clearly lacked the commitment to make the business successful and was just marking time until retirement. In fact, she had already retired, but failed to inform the rest of the company. The other manager, who had been there a number of years, appeared to have a good attitude, yet the owner was convinced that this individual had done a poor job in communicating effectively with other members of the management team.

As the profit management process progressed, the management team became more and more excited and enthusiastic about improving the bottom line. They pulled together, perhaps for the first time in years, to help this business maximize its financial success. One of the problem individuals (the one who had already "retired," but hadn't "told" her employer) showed no concern for the business's profits and was unwilling to change her behavior. The other "problem" individual who had difficulty in communicating became a significant contributor of profit ideas because the Profit Super Bowl provided a process in which he could participate in a nonthreatening environment.

Most members of the profit management team bonded together in a way the CEO had never experienced in the history of this company. What was the result? The person who was uncommitted to profit*ability* left within a few months. The commitment of the CEO to make profits flushed this unsupportive manager out of the company. The other potential problem manager learned to communicate his ideas and to be an effective manager. This business, with the efforts of its management team, turned the corner. It went from a $200,000 loss to a $300,000 profit in 12 months—a $500,000 positive change.

Why did this happen? It happened because the owner and managers became a Profit Team willing to change their attitudes and their ways of doing business. This company has been involved in the Profit Enhancement Process for seven years. Here are the results: substantial profits in each of the years they held a Profit Super Bowl and losses in the two years in which they weren't involved in the profit process. They have now learned that PEP has a significant bottom-line effect on their business. It works! They now have the profit*ability* to continue producing greater financial results, limited only by their new ideas.

Here are a few examples of the kinds of profit ideas these profit*able* people come up with now. The Profit Team, in analyzing purchasing practices, realized the company needed a qualified purchasing manager whose job was to contain costs. They hired such a person, and one of her first ideas was to go to the source to buy raw materials instead of paying a middle- man. The company actually bought the mineral rights to aggregate fields. The result: $300,000 in potential profits annually.

There was no sales manager. The Profit Team came up with the idea of semi-monthly sales meetings with the CEO (who is acting as the sales manager of this company). Without any additional expense, they were able to generate new sales leads and discuss current prospects and accounts. They established benchmarks for their sales team, each one setting six goals for themselves that had to be specific, measurable and challenging. Incentives were put into place to "super charge" everyone. They met their goals. Regular sales meetings produced sales goals that generated an extra $120,000 in profits that year.

The Profit Team looked into their inventory control. Excess inventory was costing them about two percent a month, a huge cost. They decided to hold an inventory close-out sale, and even contacted their suppliers who added consigned merchandise of their own to the sale. The company cleared out its unwanted inventory and generated an extra $60,000. The excess inventory that didn't sell was donated to charity. Because the fair market value was greater than cost, they received a nice tax deduction of cost plus 50 percent of the difference between fair market value and what they paid for the donated inventory, as permitted under tax law.

One of the Profit Team's most creative ideas was to develop the "24-Hour Customer Response Program." The team realized that they were losing market share because they weren't providing what we call "World Class Service"— doing whatever you do so well that whoever you do it for, asks for more. This "24 Hour" campaign gave customers just what they wanted. The company ordered brightly colored pins with "24" imprinted on top of their logo and gave one to every employee. They were requested to wear it daily. When a customer asked, "What does that mean?" the employee proudly replied, "It means that within 24 hours our company will take care of whatever you request from us courteously, efficiently, and accurately." This campaign built the company's reputation for being extremely attentive to their customers' requests. Can you imagine everyone in your organization repeating several times a day, "Within 24 hours our company will take care of whatever you request from us courteously, efficiently, and accurately?" It will change the culture of your business as it did this client's.

The Profit Team analyzed the company's discount policy. In fact, they found that there was no uniform discount policy. No one followed up on whether those businesses that were granted an extra discount actually increased their business activity from the company afterwards. Discounts were tightened and controls put in place. The result: more realized profits!

The Profit Team eliminated the company's practice of permitting contractors to go into their "self-service" yard and pick up their own merchandise. This effort alone generated an extra $75,000 by reducing inventory shortages. This is just one success story. You can create one, too. You *can* achieve greater financial success for your business.

---

Transform your management team into a powerhouse Profit Team.

---

For your business to change, three things must happen.

**1**—You, as head coach, owner, top financial officer, department or division head, must recognize that your company has not reached its true profit potential.

**2**—You must accept the fact that old ways of looking at ideas won't uncover new profit possibilities.

**3**—You must transform your management team into a powerhouse Profit Team.

Everyone in your business must become a possibility thinker. Change is a critical element in every business. Patience is a modern day excuse for not performing at higher levels. If you are patiently awaiting future events before initiating changes, you are harming your company by not capitalizing on tomorrow's opportunities today. It was Yogi Berra who said that "if you always do what you have always done, you'll always get what you've already got."

---

Take the ball and create new profit opportunities, become profit possibility thinkers, execute well, and score in the profit zone. Remember, if you don't know where you are going, it doesn't matter which direction you travel.

---

Just think about the profit possibilities you'll unleash when you create a profit culture within your company. Think about the possibilities of pooling all the great new profit ideas your team will begin to generate into a comprehensive, new Profit Plan for action. Think of all the profit projects your team will carry out. Think of all the profit possibilities and don't stop until you've got at least *100 Ways to Prosper in Today's Economy* (Barry Schimel's first book).

Here are some more examples of profit initiatives other clients have put in place. . .

- A manufacturer changed the composition of a portion of its sales force from commissioned sales to merchandising specialists. These specialists created better point-of-purchase displays which increased their customers' sales. Also, profits increased because the sales force focused on new business development rather than maintaining existing accounts. This resulted in $250,000 annually in potential recurring profits from additional sales.

- An automobile dealership developed a reactivation program to re-establish relationships with service department customers who hadn't used their services for a year. This resulted in $725,000 in profit potential.

- A nonprofit association reduced the paper size used for their national publication by 1/8 of an inch and "found" an extra $18,000 in recurring annual profit. (By cutting 1/8 inch, the publication could be printed on an economical standard-size paper instead of the expensive special-order paper.)

- A manufacturer installed a process to eliminate billing omissions on last-minute orders. These rush orders were usually handwritten and were not always entered into the computerized accounts receivable system. The estimated profit potential from this initiative? $180,000.

- A retail tire company established a "Red Carpet Service" to provide pick up and delivery service for people who could not take the time to get away from their office to purchase tires. Estimated recurring annual profit potential: $100,000.

---

PEP is the profit-making process for the future. Financial statements only report the scores from last season—they represent the present value of the past, not the future value of tomorrow's profit opportunities.

---

How can your company get this kind of profit*ability*? How can you turn people from task-oriented to profit-oriented—for the good of everyone in the business or organization? How do you get them to give you the new ideas that will add to the company's bottom line? And how do you accomplish those ideas so they make money for your business?

In 1989 when the economy was not healthy, we had the chance to sit around a table with a group of top CEOs. We asked them what they expected from their CPA firms, their business advisors. Were we ever surprised! Almost every one of these top executives complained that their CPA firms, for the most part, did little more than fill out tax forms and prepare financial statements. They performed mostly compliance services. They reported past transgressions, alerting them about what they had done wrong in the past (you've seen this in the management letter you receive from your accounting firm), but did not offer them ideas for being more financially successful in the future. Their advisors were stuck back in history, looking at their past scoreboard—without really appreciating what could be done to make the plays of the future. Of course, much of what accountants do is mandated by regulatory authorities and their profession. But these top entrepreneurs wanted more. They wanted new ideas. We learned from them that the loneliest place in any organization is at the top. There is no one to turn to.

We decided then and there to change the way clients are served. At the same time, we set out to change the hearts and minds of their advisors. That's the moment the Institute of Profit Advisors was born. Barry gave up a successful accounting practice to devote full time to uncovering ingenious methods of finding hidden profits in businesses of all kinds. Now approximately 100 change-ready business advisory firms are trained and licensed through the Institute of Profit Advisors to coach clients to new profit heights through the Profit Enhancement Process. Their coaching adds value to their client's business and focuses the entire organization right on the bottom line. Businesses throughout the U.S., as well as the U.K., are the beneficiaries. These firms have made the quantum leap from keeping score to making the plays.

---

Take the profit pledge.

---

Before we start, let's make sure your company is change-ready. Take a moment to answer these questions. This is a quiz that helps us determine whether prospective clients will be successful with the Profit Enhancement Process. Now you take it. It will provide you with your first hints about areas for discovering unrealized bottom line potential in your organization.

## The Are-You-Ready-for-Greater-Profit*ability* Quiz

1. Where is your profit on a scale of 1 to 10 (1 is lowest and 10 is highest)? (Describe your thoughts.)

______________________________________________

______________________________________________

______________________________________________

*Many businesses start out below 5. That leaves a lot of unrealized bottom line potential—the difference between the profit you are now achieving and what your business can achieve.*

2. Does your company have a Profit Plan? (This is different from a business plan, you'll find.) (Describe your thoughts.)

______________________________________________

______________________________________________

______________________________________________

*Don't worry, few do. But think what having a Profit Plan might mean to your business. Present it to a banker or investor and it can mean all the difference between receiving funding for your business or being strapped for cash. If you are planning to sell out in a few years, every "extra dollar of profit" you earn may add five to even ten dollars of market value to your company.*

3. Does your firm set sales targets that include gross profit objectives? (Describe your thoughts.)

______________________________________________

______________________________________________

______________________________________________

*Many businesses set sales targets, but fail to understand the real costs for achieving them.*

4. Does your business take its long-term objectives into account in its hiring process? (Describe your thoughts.)

______________________________________________

______________________________________________

______________________________________________

*Often companies hire reactively rather than objectively. Now you'll need to hire "possibility thinkers" who become part of the Profit Enhancement Process.*

5. Are the people on your staff willing to accept change? (Describe your thoughts.)

________________________________________

________________________________________

________________________________________

*Are your employees too busy working to make profits? Is your organization set in rigid patterns that don't invite new ideas and their implementation? How many new ideas from your employees are waiting on your desk right now for your consideration? Do your employee manuals even mention the word* profit?

6. What is the culture of your organization? (Describe your thoughts.)

________________________________________

________________________________________

________________________________________

*Do you know that you know all there is to know about running your business profit*ably*? Do you know that you don't know everything? Or do you not know that you don't know everything about reaching your profit potential? Are you open to new ways of doing business, new ways of thinking, new strategies for facing the challenges of the future?*

7. Do you realize that your employees are your business's most valuable asset? (Describe your thoughts.)

________________________________________

________________________________________

________________________________________

*Your carefully scouted employees should be your most valuable players. They have the ideas for adding hundreds of thousands of dollars—maybe even millions—to your company's bottom line if you unleash their profit*ability. *These people deal with your cus-*

*tomers and your vendors and your production processes every day. They know where the problems and the opportunities are, but they may not know how to tell you what they are. Are you willing to provide a nonthreatening forum for offering new ideas? Are you willing to reward your employees who put their most significant profit initiatives into action? Are you willing to get rid of your organization's sacred cows?*

8. Has your organization determined how the demand for your products or services may change based on the economy, competition and customer needs?
(Describe your thoughts.)

___

___

___

*The Profit Enhancement Process will help you get these answers by communicating effectively with your customers and vendors.*

9. Does your management team receive bonuses and/or incentives based on their performance, as well as their department's and the financial success of your business? Are there *consequences* for not meeting performance objectives?
(Describe your thoughts.)

___

___

___

*It's difficult to change. The Profit Enhancement Process requires everyone to work smarter, be more innovative and be absolutely committed to making your Profit Plan work. Bonuses and/or incentives (and they don't always have to be monetary) are absolutely essential to inspire this kind of commitment. If you aren't willing to compensate your employees, the process will not succeed in your company.*

10. Is customer service in need of improvement? Is the "bragability index" of your company higher than your competition's? Does your organization assess customer/client product and service expectations and satisfaction levels?
(Describe your thoughts.)

___

___

___

*Providing World Class Service—doing things so well that customers can't help asking for more—is essential for a successful company. It always needs improving.*

11. Does your organization work as a cohesive Profit Team?
(Describe your thoughts.)

___

___

___

*If not, PEP will inspire management teams and employee teams by pulling them together in the challenge to identify and realize profit goals. Only with every member of a company knowing what their "real" job is—enhancing the company's bottom line profits—can it reach full potential.*

12. Do you believe there is opportunity to improve the profit management of your business? (Describe your thoughts.)

___

___

___

*The Profit Enhancement Process transforms management teams into Profit Teams. Your managers must be ready to re-focus their attention from performing tasks to assisting your business in reaching its profit potential.*

13. Is your Profit Team committed to your organization's success? (Describe your thoughts.)

___

___

___

*This is very important. If everyone is not committed to the financial strategies developed during the Profit Enhancement Process, it won't work.*

14. Does your firm determine its unrealized bottom line potential by putting a dollar value on profit projects that your organization commits to undertake? (Describe your thoughts.)

______________________________________________

______________________________________________

______________________________________________

*If you can't measure it, you can't manage it. You're sure to have sales goals, but these may not be as profitable as you think. This book will teach you how to compute your unrealized bottom line potential—possibly hundreds of thousands or millions of dollars.*

15. Is there a written Profit Plan in place to achieve your organization's profit objectives?
(Describe your thoughts.)

______________________________________________

______________________________________________

______________________________________________

*If not, the Profit Enhancement Process will show you how.*

16. Are you committed to implementing new ideas if they have measurable bottom line value to your business and are in harmony with your strategic goals and objectives?
*If yes, sign your name here, and let's get started. . .*

❑ Yes, I'm ready to put the Profit Enhancement Process to work in my business.

Your signature here______________________________

# Instant Replays

In profit management, making short-term goals is as important as attaining long-term goals.

Half of the word "profit" is "pro." Is the profitability of your business PROfessionally managed?

Playing for profit means a new way of analyzing your team's performance.

TIMES x TIMES x TIMES = Endless Profit Opportunities

Admit it. You're really in business to make profits —no matter what you make or do. It's okay to use the "P" word—Profits!

Develop your bottom-line vision. You must first see it to capture it.

The most successful leaders are those whose people state, "We did it ourselves," when the work is completed.

Transform your management team into a powerhouse Profit Team.

Take the ball and create new profit opportunities, become profit possibility thinkers, execute well, and score in the profit zone. Remember, if you don't know where you are going, it doesn't matter which direction you travel.

PEP is the profit-making process for the future. Financial statements only report the scores from last season—they represent the present value of the past, not the future value of tomorrow's profit opportunities.

Take the profit pledge.

## Chapter 2

# UNDERSTANDING THE GAME

We know that we have employees who are highly skilled and experienced and who could contribute a great deal to our bottom line profitability—if they would work with us as a team. However, to get them to work with us as members of a team focusing on the broader success of the company, we knew we had to persuade them that we are committed to the success of the company and that we are open to hearing their criticism and concerns. We had to be open to the negative to draw out the positivity and creativity of our employees.

– Robert Funk, President/CEO, EKA Health & Mobility Systems

This thought expresses one of the major issues clients ask us to help them with—how do you get your employees to feel such a part of the team that they offer their ideas freely and work their hardest to help you succeed? And how do you transform managers into leaders capable of coaching their own particular group or team of players?

Again, we turn to football for the answer. Our good friend, Larry Pecattiello, Defensive Coordinator for the Detroit Lions, would make a great CEO after his years of coaching. He knows how to bring out the best in his players, and he knows that is how to win the game.

It was Larry who gave us the idea for the model to start new ideas flowing in any organization. He was telling us one day about a typical pre-game coaches' meeting when he was an assistant coach with the Washington Redskins under the great Joe Gibbs. Larry says that Joe encouraged all the coaches to offer their ideas and play strategies during discussions, based on their knowledge of the strengths and weaknesses of the players in their area of expertise—whether offense, defense, or special teams. They reviewed films of the competition and of their own team, and built the game plan together. Joe Gibbs listened to all their ideas and was always the master facilitator and final arbitrator. And no matter how heated the discussions during the session, by the end of meeting, all the coaches were committed to the game plan and ready to introduce it to the players. They were united.

This seemed like a ready-made model for the business world, where employees are the most-valued players and the best managers are the coaches who can inspire them to give their best ideas and their best hours to "winning" profits for the success of the business. So with football as our model, we developed the Profit Enhancement Process. Here's how it will work for your business.

---

Profit is always a journey; it's never a destination.

---

We all know how many financial reports we receive. They pile up at the end of every month waiting for interpretation. We attend meetings with *this* department and *that* project team. Financial and industry publications arrive on our desks by the score. What does it all mean? And how can this information be useful in our own business or organization? We all know that we can't manage it unless we can measure it. (Actually we can't manage it unless we DO manage it!)

We developed the Profit Enhancement Process so businesses will capture previously unrealized profits through an identification process and then teamwork. The process is an organized system for focusing Profit Team members in the organization on ways to turn their ideas and inside knowledge into improved financial results. It breaks the entire process into controlled, measurable profit projects that add an element of fun and excitement to the organization as each project's goal is achieved or, in many cases, surpassed. In other words, PEP is a way to identify and capture your organization's previously unrecognized and *unrealized bottom line potential.*

The Profit Enhancement Process measures the only things that can be measured in the business world:

(1) Revenues,
(2) Costs,
(3) Quality,
(4) Quantity, and
(5) Time.

These areas must be measured and measured and measured to discover hidden profits and develop a Profit Plan for transforming profit ideas into bottom line results.

Here are the five steps that will help your entire organization become profit-focused for the future so that everyone in the company benefits.

---

Step #1 in the Profit Enhancement Process is to create a culture where profit will thrive.

---

You've begun the work on this step by picking up this book! A shrewd head football coach knows that if his team is not winning or attaining its goals, something needs to change. He will look at his most important asset—his coaches and players—and analyze what his competition is doing, then change. Best of all, he will ask his coaches and players what they can be doing better. He will begin to share some of the heavy responsibility for winning with the whole team.

---

Ask yourself what's impossible to do in your business today that will make your business more profitable tomorrow?

---

This may be the most important question you ever ask in your business life.

There are three classical phases of growth in business. Phase One is an emerging business, struggling to be profitable. Everyone is working as hard as they can, but profits stagnate because many other things are necessary to make it successful. The business is experimenting with the products or services it can sell best and the marketing strategies necessary to generate those sales. This company either succeeds or goes out of business. Its key strength is the energy and entrepreneurial spirit of its founders.

Phase Two, companies exist only if they survive Phase One. They concentrate on efforts to repeat successful sales and new marketing strategies. Rapid growth occurs by developing niches and finding market opportunities that accelerate sales. Establishing sales processes and support systems are a substantial part of the second phase of growth. Profits are necessary to develop the support systems required to move the company towards its next phase.

Eventually, a business grows as much as it can by using its previous success models. Profits flatten and revenue growth becomes stagnant. New opportunities must be created to improve the bottom line and increase market share. This triggers the third phase of growth.

Compare IBM and Apple. Which company was able to change its profit culture and find new ways to compete in the business? IBM was able to change, Apple is trying hard. Think about the American automobile business over the last decade. It has been able to adapt to many markets, not just the big gas- guzzling American market of the past. Most manufacturers have pared down their expensive labor costs and moved their plants to less expensive areas of the country or the world, introduced new technology, and adapted model designs to the needs of their customers in each market segment. They've adapted to a changed marketplace and saved the American automobile industry. They heeded what Henry Ford once said, "Failure is only the opportunity to begin again, more intelligently."

Changing its ways from the way a company has done business in the past is vital for remaining financially competitive. PEP helps CEOs and managers analyze what changes are necessary to get those profits and sales to reach their potential and continue into the future. PEP will help you redesign the way you do business when the old models and methods are not producing the improved financial results you know are possible.

Most successful companies go through the first two phases, then commit to change when moving into Phase Three. This phase is most challenging because it gives entrepreneurs the opportunity to reinvent their business and maximize their sales and profit*ability*. They must be successful in this phase or else the business will continue to lose its forward motion.

No matter what phase your business is in, PEP is valuable, but particularly in Phase Two. This is the stage where change is very important. A football team's coaches don't decide on a new game plan when there are only two minutes left to go in the game. By Phase Three, a business has often lost its momentum, and its ability to change is far more difficult to achieve. It's at that moment that change is mandatory and when profit coaching is most needed. There is no luxury of time, just a sense of urgency.

There are a lot of businesses with profits of two to three percent of sales, but very few that reach 10 percent. What if a stagnant business were able to engage and empower all its employees to come up with ideas and initiatives that would reduce costs by just 10 percent? That business could almost double its profits. Do the math yourself. Let's say your revenues are one million dollars, your costs are $900,000 and you're earning a nice $100,000 a year profit. What if you were able, with attention and intention, to cut your costs by just 10 percent? You would add $90,000 to your bottom line! In other words, your profits would nearly double (hypothetically speaking) with less effort than nearly doubling your sales.

Many businesses leave considerable profits on the table, because the management team is not focused on identifying exploitable profit opportunities and just hasn't been coached to improve financial performance. How many businesses in America send their managers to courses on generating greater profit*ability*? How many managers read books on profits? Just because a company knows how to make bricks, doesn't mean it knows how to make bricks for profit. Just because a law firm knows how to service its clients' legal problems, doesn't mean it knows how to boost its bottom line. The technical work of the business is just the beginning.

As a good profit coach, like a good football coach, you can provide the forum for your employees to discover the unrealized profit opportunities in their own departments and the organization. So, Step #1 is to change your focus to the bottom line and share the responsibility for profit*ability* with your Profit Team. They'll help you come up with great new profit-enhancing ideas as soon as they begin to understand the almost limitless bottom line possibilities. One good idea will lead to another, then another, then another when they learn that profit achievements are more important than traditional responsibilities.

---

Profit Team leaders and members know that their job is to identify financial opportunities and be responsible for turning their ideas into bottom line results.

---

A hospital outpatient clinic found it was running out of space and was about to invest in a brand new and costly physical therapy facility and hire additional physical therapists for its growing number of patients needing these services. They were experiencing increased demand for more patient appointments, but were limited by treatment rooms and available staff. During the Profit Super Bowl, it was discovered that the hospital had an appointment scheduling problem. There were a lot of cancellations and fluctuations in scheduling.

The Profit Team leader given the responsibility for studying this problem discovered that most cancellations occurred during certain predictable times of the day, week, and year, including holidays. The outpatient clinic adopted a booking plan similar to the one used by airlines. They began to overbook appointments based on the statistical trends of no-shows. The result was that more patients could be accommodated, and there was no need to either increase staff or add facilities. Rather than building a new facility to handle the overflow times, they learned to schedule the appointments more systematically—and saved the hospital millions in capital expenditures on a new facility with minimal increases in personnel expenses. The interesting point is that the scheduling data was available all along, but no one had thought to use it. It took the Profit Super Bowl to provide the nonthreatening forum where the problem (an opportunity turned inside out) was identified. A manager was appointed to solve it and devise a strategy for a profit*able* solution.

---

Fleeing fortunes are the result of years of denial of significant profit opportunities.

---

Read this sentence again and tell us how many letter f's you see. Most people, even our editor, see only four; but there are really seven! The reason is that people have been conditioned to read the word *of* as if the f were a v. We have difficulty seeing the f's. This process will teach you to see every "f" in your business. It's missing the little things and doing the little things right that make all the difference.

---

Step #2 is to conduct a Profit Audit of your business.

---

Like a good coach, your next step is to analyze where your business stands today and develop priorities based on what you find. You need to do a complete *Profit Audit* of your business. This audit should delve into all aspects of your business with a focus on five key areas:

(1) Employees,
(2) Organizational Structure,
(3) Sales and Marketing,
(4) Operations, and
(5) Financial Management.

---

Businesses are drowning in information but are thirsty for knowledge.

---

Start with a review of your financial statements and corporate records, such as tax returns, mission/vision statements, annual reports, organizational chart, personnel manuals, operations and procedures manuals, and promotional and marketing materials. Ask yourself questions about the opportunities and challenges you discover there.

Then start asking your managers and other key employees the probing questions about your business that you know need answers and solutions. We've found that 70 percent of the issues uncovered in a Profit Audit come from employees. In other words, if you've got 100 employees, about 70 are consultants just waiting to be asked. The answer is the right question. This is such a vital step in the auditing process that we've developed an employee survey of carefully selected questions which we adapt to each client's requirements. You'll find a sample of that survey in Chapter 3. In our survey, employees are asked to rank the company on a scale of 1 to 10 (10 being the highest) on a variety of issues, such as:

- Do you understand our firm's profit strategy? Can you describe it?
- What do you think the company's maximum profit potential is this year?
- Do you know the company's mission/vision? Does what you do on the job support this mission?
- Do you understand the opportunities you have to increase our firm's bottom line?
- Do you think the company identifies and eliminates redundancies in tasks?
- Do you think potential customers are aware of our products and services?
- Do you catch mistakes before they impact customers and profits?
- Can you describe the relationship of your work to the company's bottom line?

These are contemplative questions. It is vital that respondents feel free to answer the survey without repercussions. And, of course, most employees typically only know the true rank of their own areas of expertise. But their perceptions are very important to your understanding of the profit*ability* of your company. Just as the linebacker might not know how to defend every type of offense, he will appreciate the job the coaches perform—determining the likelihood of certain plays occurring and what the opposition's game plan might be.

Average your employees' rankings on these important issues and analyze just where they think your business ranks today in relationship to where it could be.

Another thing you should consider is to survey select customers to determine the "Bragability Index" of your company. This is how your customers rank your business today. We are successful in obtaining a response rate of over 70 percent for our clients who ask us for help with this survey. A comprehensive survey includes questions on the organization's administration, communications, products/services and sales/marketing. Each category offers a series of detailed questions and statements that provide in-depth information about how your customers view your firm and your products or services. A sample of these questions follows:

1. *On an overall basis, how satisfied are you with our company?*

2. *Would you purchase products or services from our company again?*

3. *Would you recommend our company to other prospective customers?*

4. *How satisfied are you in your dealings with our company as a business partner?*

5. *How satisfied are you with our company's overall communication efforts?*

6. *When you think of quality products and services, do you think of our company first?*
7. *How satisfied are you with the delivery of our products and services?*
8. *Do our sales representatives keep you well-informed about our new products or services?*
9. *Do you have to buy from other sources because we don't offer the products you need?*
10. *How satisfied are you with the warranties we provide for our products?*
11. *Do our sales representatives thoroughly know and understand our products and services?*
12. *Do our sales representatives suggest solutions to improve your business?*
13. *How satisfied are you with the personal commitment of our sales representatives?*
14. *How satisfied are you with the commitment of our company's management to assist you?*
15. *Can you always promptly contact someone in our company who will make decisions that affect you?*

The results of these customer surveys, impartially analyzed, will help you identify a list of profit issues you will want addressed right away and others to be addressed over time.

---

"Traditional budgeting is a waste of time!"
–Former Accountant turned Profit Advisor

---

Traditionally, budgeted profit is computed by subtracting budgeted overhead expenses and budgeted cost of sales from budgeted sales. More often than not, those figures are based on historic information without the insights gained through profit*ability*. By conducting a Profit Audit, potential profit will be revealed in a more realistic and meaningful way and quantified into a profit*ability* budget.

- Sales projections will be based on the number of customers, the frequency of customer transactions, and how much customers are willing to pay for each transaction.

- Selling price will be based upon customers' perceptions of value as well as eliminating preconceived, market-defined price barriers. In part, the value customers perceive will be based on the support and world-class service they feel they receive. Customers will happily pay greater prices for *value* when they feel your product or service has equaled or exceeded their expectations.

---

The customer never says your prices are too high. They say the value of what they received is too low.

---

In the 1980s, you may have increased revenues by selling more and raising prices. Today, the greater your price—unless value is given—the more reason you give your customers to look for alternative suppliers. Your customers actually set your sales prices based on their perception of how valuable they believe your products and services to be.

When you create greater perceived value, you have the opportunity to raise your prices (within limits, of course). Costs that are necessary to enhance perceived value are essential and include costs of goods sold, assuming your customers perceive value in what you produce. Overhead is not valued by your customers unless they understand it and get value from the service and function it provides; i.e., timely billing, timely response, clean and exceptional facility, and so on. Overhead expenses—such as insurance, office supplies, permits and licenses, and accounting departments—do not have perceived value to your customers, but you can't operate without them. So make sure your customers understand how valuable what you sell is to them and that includes the "whole" business.

---

Consider not only the well-executed plays, but also the profit "fumbles."

---

Ah, yes, you must consider the negatives or profit "fumbles." Did your survey indicate your employees don't understand the Big Picture, and that they lack knowledge and training on how to make the business more successful? Did your customers say their orders were completed without mistakes? Did the majority of your employees say that they don't understand the company's mission and where they fit into it? Did they say they need further training to do their jobs with more profit*ability*? These are all fumbled plays. We call them "profit fumbles." They cause lower profits, but they can be identified. They can be measured, and they can be eliminated, reduced or improved via the Profit Enhancement Process.

Try to assign a negative dollar figure to these trouble areas. Quantify, quantify, quantify. Know the numbers. It's the language of business! Here's how:

(1) Assign a negative value to each of the "fumbles" you know have a negative impact on your profit*ability*. Think of these fumbles as all the words that start with *mis, re,* and *un*. Here is a list of the kinds of "fumbles" that could be keeping your team out of the profit zone.

| **Mis** | **Re** | **Un** |
|---|---|---|
| Misunderstood | Restock | Unclear |
| Mistakes | Retrain | Undone |
| Missed deadlines | Redo | Unkept promise |
| Mismanaged | Redeliver | Unnecessary |
| Misplaced | Reposition | Unfocused |

It's these kinds of issues that send customers away in a huff, cost the company unplanned-for expenses in having to redo or remake, and result in a warehouse full of unsold inventory.

Profit fumbles are costly problems. Detecting problems means identifying and measuring recurring expenses. Preventing problems equals recurring profits. The choice is yours. These are the costly issues, the challenges, that your Profit Audit will identify. Once you have recognized them, it is possible, in many cases, to eliminate them through the Profit Enhancement Process.

(2) Now look at your Income Statement in a new way:

| | **OLD Traditional Presentation** | | **NEW Non-traditional Profit Fumbler Presentation** |
|---|---|---|---|
| Sales | XXX | Sales | XXX |
| Less Costs of Sales | <XXX> | Less Costs of Sales | <XXX> |
| Gross Profit | XXX | Gross Profit | XXX |
| Less Overhead | <XXX> | Less Overhead | <XXX> |
| | < N/A >① | Less; Profit Fumbles | <XXX>② |
| Net Profits | XXX | Net Profits | XXX |

① *Unidentified and unmeasured profit fumbles are buried in lower sales and inflated cost of sales and overhead.*

② *Profit fumbles are identified and measured and available for instant replay to allow the coach and the Profit Team to improve the system and/or the process towards constant and never-ending improvement.*

As you can see, this is a meaningful way to identify your profit potential opportunities. It helps you understand the toll those negative "profit fumbles" take on your bottom line.

We agree with the assessment of Jack Welch, CEO of American giant General Electric, on the budgeting process:

> The budget is the bane of corporate America. It never should have existed. A budget is this: if you

make it, you generally get a pat on the back and a few bucks. If you miss it, you get a stick in the eye —or worse. Making a budget is an exercise in minimalization. You're always trying to get the lowest out of people, because everyone is negotiating to get the lowest number.

The Profit Enhancement Process creates predictable bottom line results that look toward the future. Standard budgeting produces probable results based on the past. And the past does not equal the future of a profit*able* business.

---

Profit fumbles are really opportunities to score… in disguise.

---

Put the fumbles together with the opportunities you've uncovered and your Profit Audit will offer you a real menu of options and issues to be addressed. It will give you the opportunity to see the letter f's that were previously hidden to you, and a checklist of actions you consider most important for the future of your company—not just some projected figures based on the past.

Now prioritize the issues in your Profit Audit, identifying six to ten of the best that you would like to tackle first. These are the issues you will want to bring to what we call the Profit Super Bowl.

---

Step #3 is to hold a profit management retreat— a Profit Super Bowl—where managers and employees become your powerhouse Profit Team.

---

Just as the head coach calls his assistant coaches together to analyze the previous season and to formulate a game plan for the future, your next step in the Profit Enhancement Process is to call your Profit Team together. Now it's time to share the most important ideas from the Profit Audit with your team, to get their consensus, and to begin devising strategies to address these opportunities and challenges. In football, the coaches look at films and statistics from past games and begin analyzing information. They learn what they and their opponents did right and wrong, analyze patterns of play, and begin to anticipate what they might expect next season. They begin to revise the "playbook" and devise game plans for the future. As head coach for your business, it's time for you to do the same.

---

The Profit Super Bowl turns department managers into team players.

---

The Profit Super Bowl is a profit management brainstorming/planning session rolled into one: it is your coaches' meeting. So select your "assistant coaches" well, at least one from each department, or from each region if yours is a larger company. Try to limit the number to no more than about 20. More than this makes the meeting too unwieldy. Make sure the people you invite are willing to put forth the effort to make a profit difference for your company. Make sure they really want to coach and have the ability to do so.

During this retreat, the goal is to convert your Company Team into a Profit Team. How do you do this? Provide a free forum of ideas, away from the office, with no complaints, no criticisms, no hashing over old times. This game is not about the past, it's about the future that begins right now. This is a meeting where the backed-up dam of ideas locked in each team player's head is released, considered, quantified, and put into place in the new Profit Plan if warranted.

When we hold such Profit Super Bowls for our clients, the length of time is tailored to our client's need list. Our role is multifaceted. We act as the facilitators. The CEO's role is to listen intently and yet participate as freely as his team players. One or two days seems the right amount of time necessary to facilitate an in-depth discussion of top issues. This also allows time for bringing out additional issues for group discussion. Now is when you'll get the group's consensus for implementing profit strategies. It is important that the Profit Plan be developed with the consensus of the Profit Team. People do not resist their own ideas, but they may resent and then resist other people's ideas that are imposed upon them.

You must demonstrate support for the Profit Team members in their efforts to improve the company's bottom line. Above all, you must create an atmosphere where real problems can be discussed without fear of retribution. Profit Team members should realize their value to the business and learn that each and every one of them is in charge of profit. As profit strategies are discussed, the Profit Team must reach a consensus on which are to be accepted for the Profit Plan. For each accepted strategy, a team leader (or Profit Champion) should be appointed with responsibility for "carrying the ball" for that strategy and mastering the play that will take it over the goal line. If it's everyone's job, it's no one's job, and the project will fumble. But with one staunch champion to run with it, the play could lead to a profit touchdown!

Suddenly, you'll all see the Profit Plan begin to unfold before you. A real sense of Profit Team cohesion will be developing. There will be excitement in the air.

---

Step #4 is to take all those good ideas and build the Profit Plan—your company's game plan for winning big over the next season.

---

Besides building profit*ability*, the Profit Super Bowl is the time when your company's plan for profit will emerge. As the attendees define specific profit initiatives—some for eliminating profit fumbles, others for implementing new strategies—Profit Team members are coached to quantify a dollar amount that could be added to the company's bottom line with completion of each profit strategy. Why spend $1,000,000 to make $100,000? Why not spend $100,000 to make $1,000,000? This computation involves enumerating the financial assumptions upon which that estimate is based—the projected income less the costs associated with the profit initiative. This is difficult for Profit Team members to comprehend, but it is essential because it helps the Profit Team understand the financial implications of a profit generating idea. This estimate may then be tweaked some by the Profit Team to make it more conservative, thus more credible as it is internalized by the team.

Step #4 takes place when these financial strategies are totaled and the actual unrealized bottom line potential of the business is revealed. Each strategy has a financial goal. Without financial goals, profits will not occur. Expectations create results. This figure can be hundreds of thousands to millions of dollars. The unrealized bottom line potential is much more meaningful than a budget. In fact, businesses need to revise their budgets when they determine their unrealized bottom line potential. This is where your Profit Plan is transformed into a quantitative goal for "Super Bowl" profits. The unrealized bottom line potential is activity-based and results-driven. Its financial goals are based on future opportunities. It is very different from a budget which is based on past performance. Now you will have a never-before-realized confidence in your company's profit*ability*.

---

Accountability and responsibility will create greater profit*ability* and prevent early retirement.

---

With your Profit Plan in writing and accountability assigned for its many profit projects, everyone has a sense of what they can do to enhance the bottom line. As Dana Stubblefield said when he left the San Francisco 49ers for the Washington Redskins:

> Each year, the 49ers believe they're going to the Super Bowl. It doesn't matter who's wearing the uniforms. There's a level that's expected of you, and if you don't reach it, they'll find someone else. That's the attitude we need around here—the attitude that says, "We're going to win every game." If I can help the guys here get that attitude, I will have accomplished something.

That's the kind of attitude you should expect from your Profit Super Bowl, and what you want to hear from every one of your new Profit Champions or project leaders.

Your next step is to appoint your top "assistant coach" to work most closely with the team during the profit process. This Profit Activities Leader or PAL could be the COO, CFO or senior vice president of your company, someone who shares your vision for the company, understands the big financial picture, and will help you guide the entire process over the financial goal line. Your Profit Activities Leader should also be a good coach who is skilled in helping each individual team member "play" his or her best to reach their genuine profit*ability* level.

**Characteristics of a Profit Activities Leader:**

- Develops self-motivating Profit Team leaders.
- Gets Profit Team leaders to carry out their own ideas for greater profit*ability*.
- Creates Profit Teams that manage the bottom line.
- Encourages Profit Team members, working effectively with other departments, to advance the bottom line of the entire organization.
- Instills "World-Class Service." This creates change that enhances the bottom line and advances the mission of the organization.

---

Step #5 is to play the Profit Game to win.

---

The world is full of great ideas that never went anywhere because they were not implemented well. In football, the players and coaches refer to the playbook constantly. The coaches introduce new plays during verbal presentations, in visual presentations on film and overheads, and in written form, constantly seeking player feedback for buy-in and improvement. They revise the playbook based on past experience, and an analysis of all the coaches' feedback about their competitors' winning moves. Players come to understand the reasons and strategies behind each new play and how it fits into the game plan and the team's goals for the season. Then practice begins.

During the PEP, Profit Champions form additional Profit Teams to implement their assigned profit projects. The Profit Activities Leader meets with them regularly to assess how they are doing and to hold them accountable. The job of the PAL is to make the company successful by giving Profit Champions the resources they need. Do they need more time allotted to complete the project, more staff support, assistance from other departments? Are there additional profit opportunities that have become apparent as a result of working on the projects? Is there a better idea to attain that goal? Should a project be modified to better accomplish it?

Our experience has taught us that the main reasons for the failure to implement ideas are:

- No one individual is responsible;
- Deadlines are not set, adhered to, or focused on;
- No means of measuring progress exists;
- Priorities have not been established;
- Those responsible for implementation aren't rewarded if successful or do not suffer consequences if they are not successful;
- People haven't been trained to implement profit projects; and
- Consensus was not strong enough at the start.

During the all-important implementation segment of the profit process, your Profit Activities Leader must have the authority to give Profit Champions and their committees the time and resources necessary to accomplish the profit projects. If no one is responsible for monitoring progress, it is likely deadlines will be missed. People do properly what is inspected—not just expected. Without accountability, projects will keep slipping until everyone forgets them. The PAL must be someone your team respects and who is empowered by the CEO to ensure that ideas identified by the Profit Team are carried out. Profit strategies need the unequivocal backing of the CEO. The CEO has the right to veto any initiative, but from our experience he or she rarely does. If Profit Teams are developing strategies to make a business more successful, there is little reason to exercise the veto power. However, remember the Golden Rule of the late Jack Kent Cooke, owner of the Washington Redskins:

"The man with the gold, rules."

Initiate rewards for success and enforce consequences for not living up to the commitments, and your implementation process is destined to win. Super profits are the trophy.

As Profit Advisors, we meet regularly with our client's Profit Activities Leader to share the responsibility with him or her and to help work through the issues. There's only one way to eat an elephant: one bite at a time. We also prepare a monthly progress report to the CEO which measures, among other things, the percentage of completion for each profit project.

These are the steps in the Profit Enhancement Process. If you believe that you are already accomplishing them, try this test.

1. List five people who report to you.
2. Beside each name write five proactive profit projects that person has suggested to you in the last six months.
3. Record the date when each initiative was or will be completed, who is responsible for doing the work, and the amount of profit each will add to your bottom line.

## A TEST OF YOUR COMPANY'S CURRENT PROFIT*ABILITY*

| Employees Who Report to You | Suggested Profit Projects *(5 for each reports to you)* | Expected Completion Date | Profit Champion | $ Profit Expected |
|---|---|---|---|---|
| 1. | | | | |
| | | | | |
| | | | | |
| | | | | |
| | | | | |
| 2. | | | | |
| | | | | |
| | | | | |
| | | | | |
| | | | | |
| 3. | | | | |
| | | | | |
| | | | | |
| | | | | |
| | | | | |
| 4. | | | | |
| | | | | |
| | | | | |
| | | | | |
| | | | | |
| 5. | | | | |
| | | | | |
| | | | | |
| | | | | |
| | | | | |

If your worksheet is full of ideas that are consistently being implemented, congratulations. You are successfully following a Profit Enhancement Process of your own. If you were unable to complete this test—most business owners and managers can't—read on.

# Instant Replays

Profit is always a journey; it's never a destination.

Step #1 in the Profit Enhancement Process is to create a culture where profit will thrive.

Ask yourself what's impossible to do in your business today that will make your business more profitable tomorrow?

Profit Team leaders and members know that their job is to identify financial opportunities and be responsible for turning their ideas into bottom line results.

Fleeing fortunes are the result of years of denial of significant profit opportunities.

Step #2 is to conduct a Profit Audit of your business.

Businesses are drowning in information, but are thirsty for knowledge.

"Traditional budgeting is a waste of time!"
—Former Accountant turned Profit Advisor

The customer never says your prices are too high. They say the value of what they received is too low.

Consider not only the well-executed plays, but also the profit "fumbles."

Profit fumbles are really opportunities to score...in disguise.

The Profit Super Bowl turns department managers into team players.

Step #3 is to hold a profit management retreat—a Profit Super Bowl—where managers and employees become your powerhouse Profit Team.

The Profit Super Bowl turns department managers into team players

Step #4 is to take all those good ideas and build the Profit Plan—your company's game plan for winning big over the next season.

Accountability and responsibility will create greater profitability and prevent early retirement.

Step #5 is to play the Profit Game to win.

## Chapter 3

# PRE-SEASON TRAINING: Identifying Your Profit Audit Opportunities

By making each person involved in the program...we were able to come up with our own ideas. Ideas to save money, work smarter, and make our company a better place to work for our employees, and a better environment for our valued customers.

– Carlos B. Hart, President, Hart Motor Company, Inc.

---

You can't tackle problems unless you know what they are. You can't leap into profit opportunities until you have identified them.

---

A great football coach spends the first weeks after the season is over reviewing and revising the team's playbook— its record of every possible play the team has ever used that works. He reviews films of the winning teams' games, analyzing their formations, the areas of the field where they are effective making plays, and what they did during the first down, the second, and that crucial third. He analyzes their patterns of play and how his team might utilize some of their most successful opponents' strategies to play ever better and beat them at their own game during the next season.

---

Great profit coaches spend 33% of their time on product service and idea development, 33% on coaching, and 34% on implementing the new Profit Plan.

---

In the same way, a great CEO must start with what we call a Profit Audit—taking complete stock of the business, identifying new opportunities and old challenges. How do you do this? One way is by asking questions. Ask yourself, your customers, and your employees. The goal is to identify meaningful profit opportunities.

The Profit Audit is designed to be a systematic assessment of where the business can improve. It should delve into five key areas of every business:

(1) Employees
(2) Organizational Structure
(3) Sales and Marketing
(4) Operations
(5) Financial Management

Keep each of these areas in mind as you conduct your Profit Audit. You can get some ideas from your financial information. But these, after all, are simply scoreboards. They tell you the score at the end of the game, not how you got there, or where to go next. The most significant opportunities are locked up in the minds of those you work with.

---

Never, never, never stop asking questions.

---

This is a chapter full of questions, the kind of questions we ask when we work with a client. Questions are what help us help our clients identify the hidden profit opportunities that have made thousands, if not millions, of dollars of difference to their bottom lines. And questions are what will help you do the same.

After all our years in business, we can now drive into the parking lot of any business or organization, park, go into the reception area, walk around the office or plant, stroll through the warehouse, talk to a few employees, drive away and suggest three or four profit opportunities that weren't previously apparent to their business. Much of it is common sense and much of it is learning how to identity it. That has to come from years of experience. That's what this chapter will share with you.

---

Start your Profit Audit with a profit*ability* tour of your business.

---

Drive into your own parking lot. What do you see? Is it well maintained, no potholes, few empty spaces? But maybe there are no expensive cars parked there, and no prestige signage on buildings.

What about the reception area? Is it nice, neat and clean? Are there recent magazines available? How well is the receptionist fielding calls? Does she answer the phone abruptly? Does she sound more like a machine instead of a customer goodwill ambassador? Is she getting a predictable result from her mannerisms, ways and words? Does she seem to be referring sales inquiries to the person who can answer them and turn them into an order? What signs of smooth operations can be seen by watching the receptionist do her job? When calls are transferred, are they promptly answered or is the customer left dangling, or worse, lost in the shuffle?

When you stroll through any part of the organization, do you observe the simple clues that give you an indication of how well the company is doing?

When talking to employees, do they seem upbeat? Are they supportive of the company's policies and procedures? Do they know the company's policies and procedures? Taking an unofficial trip (with attention and intention) around any company is a real eye-opener.

We once walked into the reception area of a client who had hired us to help the company reach its profit potential. We took one look at their huge underutilized space, and came up with an idea that saved the company thousands of dollars. You guessed it. Why not rent out the part they weren't using, and use the money to improve the bottom line? Simple, yes! Profit*able*, yes! But the CEO couldn't see the obvious. He wasn't using his profit*ability*.

As a profit coach, you must be a bloodhound honing in on hidden profit opportunities.

If we were to walk into your office right now and throw a million one-dollar bills on the floor, what would you do? You'd stoop right over and pick them up, right?

In a way, that is what we are doing when we ask clients these questions. The answer to any one of them will be the creative spark for finding hidden profits.

So start your Profit Audit by asking yourself these primary questions:

(1) *Are you currently selling to enough customers?*

(2) *Are you selling enough to your current customers?*

(3) *Are your customers bragging about doing business with you?*

(4) *What can you do to increase the number of current customers?*

(5) *What can you do to increase the transaction value of each customer?*

(6) *What can you do to keep your customers coming back more often?*

(7) *What conflicts between departments influence customer satisfaction, timeliness, and/or quality?*

(8) *What redundancies occur within tasks?*

(9) *Do you have long-term, motivated, loyal employees?*

(10) *How can you increase the perceived value of your products and services so that your customers will be willing to pay you more?*

(11) *What are your customers' expectations of your business, products and services?*

(12) *What can be done to improve the process of all of the above in each departmentment and in the company as a whole?*

If you can answer these questions, you will be a long way towards identifying where your real profit opportunities are hiding. This is the essence of the Profit Audit. It's significantly more involved than these key questions, but we believe that if every business knew the answers to these basic questions, they would be ready to win the Profit Game today.

---

The Profit Audit provides you with a scouting report of profit possibilities—not answers.

---

Your audit should consist of every question you'd like answered about how your business is organized and how it operates, about those who work there, those who buy your products or services, and about the state of your finances. But all these questions, answered by you, your employees, and even your customers, won't provide you with a plan of action, a game plan. The opportunities and problems discussed during the Profit Audit are like the football coach's "scouting report"—a list of profit issues you will wish to address in your game plan for the season. The Profit Audit will make you aware of all the challenges and opportunities that your business can pursue, a menu of options, choices you never knew existed for your business. It doesn't come right out and tell you how to be more financially successful. It's your play book of possible plays. You must then decide which ones will produce the biggest payoff.

You'll need to introduce the plays to your Profit Team, toss the ball around with them, see which ones work best for your team and its players, perfect your plays with them, then you'll be ready to play ball. Just as in football, it's up to you and your managers to choose the issues you feel are most important. In order to choose the right strategies for your team and implement their ideas, you'll need to put your Profit Team to work.

---

Financial statements are
the scoreboard from last season.
Ask yourself: What can we do better next season?

---

In most cases, financial reports, your balance sheet and income statement, represent the present value of your company's past performances. They are a report card that reaffirms which strategies work and illustrates when your business is not living up to expectations. They are important, there is no doubt about that; but keep in mind the fact that there are many more clues to profit*ability* than financial information provides.

For instance, consult your trade association or franchise organization. They are in business to help you be successful, and consider themselves to be the advocate for your business. They will supply you with industry statistics and trends, access to their library of information, and invitations to their activities intended to offer opportunities for networking with others who will have profit ideas to share with you.

But, of course, for your Profit Audit you should review the following documents (always keeping the five key areas of your business in mind) and ask yourself questions like these:

**#1 - Employees**
**Personnel Manual**

- Are employees required to sign a statement acknowledging that they have received the personnel manual and understand that the rules specified govern their employment?
- Are regular employee evaluations performed to correct inappropriate behavior and to reinforce good performance?
- Are there coaching sessions between evaluations?
- Has your company protected itself from unfounded employee claims and lawsuits?
- Are you satisfied with your employee retention rate?
- Do job descriptions exist so that employees know what is expected of them?

### #2 - Organizational Structure
### Succession Plan

- If something happened to the owners of the business, is there a written succession plan?

- Key employees can be the lifeblood of your business. Are there contingency plans for filling the void if they are unable to work or were to leave the company?

### Organization Chart

- Is your organization chart complete and up-to-date?

- A person can be effective in directly managing only a limited number of people.

Do any department heads have too many people directly reporting to them? Which department heads are constantly in demand and have little time to finish projects or supervise others?

- Does a logical chain of command exist?

### #3 - Sales & Marketing
### Marketing Plan

- Many companies have not identified potential customers for their products and services. Have you developed customer profiles for your products and services? What are you doing to create interest in your products or services with these potential customers?

- It is much easier to sell more to existing customers than to find new ones. Are your customers aware of the products and services that are appropriate for their needs?

- Is your mission statement visible for customers and employees to see? Do they understand it?

- Has your mission statement been recently reviewed and is it in sync with your existing goals?

**#4 - Operations**
**Business Plan**

- Does a business plan exist?

- Are the long-term goals of your business identified, and are there action plans in place to realize them?

- Do your employees understand what your company is trying to achieve?

**Policies and Procedures Manual**

- Do you have guidelines in place to ensure production and performance standards in all areas of your business?

- Are your procedures spelled out clearly and precisely so that different people doing the same job have similar performance standards?

- Have you documented relevant policies and procedures so that there is a map for others to follow?

**#5 - Financial Management**
**Financial Statements**

- Can you explain what caused favorable results? Can you cause them to be repeated predictably?

- Can you explain unfavorable results? Can you cause them NOT to be repeated?
- In any income or expense category, can you explain why there are differences between current and prior periods? What can be done to change the results during the next period?
- Have you developed benchmarks from past financial information that will be useful in determining if you are improving in certain areas or getting worse? Are you using those benchmarks?

**Business Tax Returns**

- Have you optimized federal tax savings at the expense of state taxes?
- Have you optimized tax deductions and credits for income tax purposes?
- In a "C" corporation, donating excess inventory to certain charities can create a tax deduction greater than what you paid for the inventory. Would such a donation help this year's bottom line?
- There are tax credits available that produce significantly greater tax benefits than tax deductions. Each dollar of tax credit can save up to a dollar of tax. These credits are available for expenditures in research and development, hiring certain economically disadvantaged individuals, and various other areas. Have you pursued the significant opportunities available to you by capturing these lucrative tax credits?

### Shareholders' Tax Returns

- Have you established medical reimbursement plans to cover expenses not covered by your traditional health plans?

- Review the interest rates you are paying on your personal residence and other loans. Can the loans be restructured to give you lower interest rates and greater tax deductions?

### Compensation Plans

- Do your employees understand your compensation plan?

- Does your compensation plan motivate the type of behavior you want from employees that will result in financial gain for your company?

If you do not have the answers to these questions, you have work to do. Consider adding their development to your Profit Action Plan.

Remember that the financial information sources you use are scoreboards from previous periods. They show you where your business stands, but they don't tell you how you got there or the game plan necessary to improve the score. Suppose you have a bad quarter, and your financial statement shows a decrease in profits. Traditional financial reporting states it happened, but does not answer the most important question: Why?

There are a number of potential reasons to explain the decline. For example, your product may no longer be competitive in the marketplace, or deficiencies in customer service have alienated potential and existing customers. Late deliveries may have caused customers to seek more reliable alternative sources of supply, or your sales people may have been ineffective in their job and are either not finding new opportunities or are unable to convert existing ones into sales. Perhaps you are burdened by excessive interest, inadequate gross margin, inadequate expense control or excessive carrying costs. These are a few of the many causes of decline in profits.

When you review your financial statements, you may learn that costs have risen. In some cases, trends will be recognized and costs contained in selected areas. Most of our clients are mature and stable companies who are already doing a proficient job at cost control. In many cases, they are operating within industry-accepted norms.

So what less-obvious situations may be causing a rise in costs that are not revealed in traditional financial reports? Perhaps, equipment is outmoded and frequently breaks down. This increases labor costs, because employees can't work up to their capacity. Perhaps there are redundancies in your order fulfillment department. This increases the time and expense of getting products to your customers. Perhaps your costs are rising because certain departments are not effective. Perhaps, as happened in the late 1990s, a tight labor market may have caused labor costs to increase. Someone or some process that worked in an earlier phase of your business is no longer in sync with your present organizational goals. Employee turnover is also a major cause of increased costs and decreased sales. Besides the expense and inconvenience of finding new people, disruption in operations has a ripple effect in many other areas.

When your company has plateaued and is not making the gains you feel are possible, what do you do? Traditional financial information is the basis from which to begin asking many of the tough questions. However, this is extremely complex and difficult for someone to do who is too close to the business or industry. The longer you are with a company, the less ability you have to identify the possibilities. You can no longer see the letter "f's".

---

Ask your employees!
They know 70 percent of the answers.

---

While performing Profit Audits for our clients, we invite department heads, managers, up-and-coming all-stars, and others who have a sense of what's going on in the organization to fill out a survey specifically designed for the needs of our clients, but similar to the sample below. Employees are assured that their personal answers will not be shared with others. It is important to have honest answers, untainted by what employees think the company wants to hear. They must reflect what they really believe. Perceptions are real! When we work with a client on a Profit Audit engagement, we often have employees send their surveys directly to us to ensure confidentiality.

Here are a few sample questions from a questionnaire we use. Adapt it to your company's needs.

**The Profit Audit Questionnaire**

Name of Company________________________________________

Employee's Name______________________________ *(you can make this optional)*

Department______________________________ Date:_____________

***Instructions:*** *This questionnaire focuses on the five integral parts of a successful organization. Its purpose is to illustrate your organization's unrealized profit opportunities. For each issue, select a number between 1 and 10 that best ranks your organization's standing. One is the least and ten is the greatest. Select N/A for those questions that you think are not relevant. Base your answers on your impression of your company, and not just your department. Your answers should reflect the way things are, not the way they should be! Your answers will be kept confidential.*

***Overall Perspective:***

On a scale of 1 to 10, with 10 being your company's maximum profit potential, how do you rate your company this year?
(Circle your answer.)
1  2  3  4  5  6  7  8  9  10
What would moving several notches mean to your company's profit*ability*?
Your estimate in dollars of Profit Potential: $_______________.

### *EMPLOYEES: Section #1*

On a scale of 1 to 10, rate your company's standing with your employees in these areas:

| *Issue* | *Score* |
|---|---|
| Our employees are focused on generating profits and have a plan to follow. | ________ |
| We have thorough orientation and initial training programs. | ________ |
| Our evaluation process lets people know where they stand throughout the year. | ________ |
| We have the right people in the right jobs at the right wage. | ________ |
| Our employees know our firm's mission and vision, and their activities support its realization. | ________ |

### *ORGANIZATIONAL STRUCTURE :Section #2*

On a scale of 1 to 10, with 10 being the best, rate your company's organizational structure in these areas:

| *Issue* | *Score* |
|---|---|
| We are effective in implementing projects. | ________ |
| Up-to-date job descriptions exist and guide employees' activities. | ________ |
| We continually fix the causes of problems, instead of fighting the same fires. | ________ |
| We leverage decisions to lower staff, to free time and to maximize resources. | ________ |
| Employees put the welfare of our company ahead of their department. | ________ |

***SALES & MARKETING: Section #3***

On a scale of 1 to 10, with 10 being the best, rate your company's sales & marketing in these areas:

| ***Issue*** | ***Score*** |
|---|---|
| Potential customers are aware of our products and services. | ________ |
| We set sales targets with gross profit objectives. | ________ |
| We maximize sales from our complete product line to existing customers. | ________ |
| Our customers are easily able to obtain reliable information about their order. | ________ |
| Strong two-way communications occur between sales and other departments. | ________ |

***OPERATIONS: Section #4***

On a scale of 1 to 10, with 10 being the best, rate your company's operations in these areas:

| ***Issue:*** | ***Score*** |
|---|---|
| We meet our customers' delivery requirements. | ________ |
| Our procedures provide maximum efficiency and minimum waste. | ________ |
| We catch mistakes before they impact customers and profits. | ________ |
| A problem with our product/service is quickly and satisfactorily resolved. | ________ |
| We know our customers' expectations and satisfaction levels. | ________ |

### *FINANCIAL MANAGEMENT: Section #5*

On a scale of 1 to 10, with 10 being the best, rate your company's financial management in these areas:

| *Issue* | *Score* |
| --- | --- |
| Cash flow is good. We collect receivables and pay bills on time. | ________ |
| Our pricing strategies are based on market value. | ________ |
| We measure labor-and-equipment productivity and use the data in decision-making. | ________ |
| Flash reports of key business indicators are distributed and used on a timely basis. | ________ |
| Our inventory control achieves maximum turns and is equal to industry norms. | ________ |

When you look at the results, you'll see a pretty clear picture of how your business, or any business, measures up.

When a company scores 6 or higher in all sections, the business is well-balanced and profit*able*, but hasn't started to exploit its profit potential. Unless the business scored 8 or higher in every section, our experience suggests that there is always room to improve—and additional profit to generate.

When we perform a Profit Audit for clients, we also conduct personal interviews with management and selected employees. This might be hard for you to do because employees may feel awkward revealing their feelings to their boss. We are able to ask the Barbara Walters' type questions, the ones that cut to the chase. We assure them we will keep their individual answers confidential so they don't feel threatened. We abide by this promise because we want their message heard and don't want the messenger destroyed.

Through these questions our goal is to find out for clients further information on why their employees think as they do. We ask each employee for the reasons they gave particularly low or high scores. We listen carefully for issues each person thinks are most important. We reinforce the promise that top management is eager to hear their ideas for increasing sales and margins, improving processes, controlling costs and increasing customer satisfaction.

Our questions always begin with: "What do you think your company is trying to accomplish?" The answers are amazing. What we're looking for here is their ideas about where the company may be missing some profit opportunities, and whenever an issue is stated, we ask for examples.

Our next question always is: "What is holding your company back from getting to the next profit plateau?"

After exploring the answer to this vital question, we continue with questions like:

- Why did you join the company, and what has influenced you to stay?
- What would you identify as your organization's greatest strengths?
- What additional strengths do you think your company must develop to remain competitive?
- What would you identify as your organization's greatest weaknesses?
- How do you think you could eliminate these weaknesses to remain competitive?
- What does your company do better than any other?
- What unique value do you provide to customers?

- How can you increase that value next year?
- What new markets could you explore?
- Which current products or services do you think should be eliminated and why?
- Do you know what your competition does better than you?
- Who do you think your competitors will be in the future?
- Does your department have all the resources it needs to be successful?
- What business issues do you think management should concentrate on?

You may be able to gain enough knowledge of what your employees are thinking from the written survey. If not, try some of these personal interviews. It's not easy, especially if there is some distance between management and employees. You may need to assign these interviews to another level of management or to the Profit Advisor.

---

Create a profit opportunities checklist of the issues you've discovered and pick the top ten. These are the first plays your Profit Team should consider practicing.

---

Once you've gathered this information, make a list of all the profit opportunities and challenges you've discovered. Don't stop asking questions. Challenge yourself to consider all sorts of issues that could optimize your company's profit potential. But start by selecting the top ten profit opportunities based on what you think should be done first. Once these have been addressed, another ten or so can be tackled by your Profit Teams.

After we perform a Profit Audit for a client, we offer a comprehensive list of possible "options" or profit plays which the CEO has not been able to see. We put this list into the Profit Opportunities Report. These plays hold the keys to moving the company forward toward the profit zone.

In our Profit Opportunities Reports, we raise profit-probing issues. A brief sample follows:

**Revenue**

Have you considered training your customer service employees to sell all the company's products or services, not just those from their own department?

Are your sales people using low prices as the main tool to maintain customer loyalty?

Should you initiate a process to identify customers' expectations and the types of services necessary to satisfy them?

Should you have a lead-generation system?

Do you think your prices match the value your customers believe they are worth?

**Gross Margins**

Can selected prices be raised now?

Do you have mechanisms in place to regularly evaluate pricing levels and make appropriate changes?

Have you considered announcing future price increases to create additional sales in the current period?

Can you unbundle your products and services and charge more in total?

What is your criterion for accepting low or unprofit*able* sales? Should they be eliminated?

Have you determined which sales are unprofit*able*, and what should be done to make them more profit*able* or eliminate them altogether?

**Operating Expenses**

Are you spending enough on sales and marketing? Reduced sales may be a result of not committing reasonable resources to advertising and marketing.

Should the procurement of supplies for all locations be consolidated to get better prices and terms?

Are vendors asked for ideas to help control expenses, services or supply alternatives?

Can maintenance contracts be renegotiated and/or eliminated?

**Employee Issues**

Is overtime being controlled? When is it approved?
Are bonuses based on incentives? Are bonuses subjective or objective?

Have you considered varying the deductible amount from compensation for health insurance, based on employee compensation?

Have you considered upward evaluations of management?

**Inventory**

Is your management of inventory as effective as it should be?

Do you have a regular system for eliminating slow moving inventory? The average monthly cost of carrying inventory is two percent.

### Fixed Assets

Have you considered a process to regularly measure the sensibility of keeping old equipment vs. acquiring new?

### Notes Payable

Instead of receiving interest income from the bank, have you thought about paying down your line of credit since this more than doubles your yield?

### Corporate Tax Matters

Have you considered investing in domestic dividend-paying companies and/or mutual funds? "C" corporations are entitled to a 70-percent dividend exclusion.

### Personal Tax Matters

Have you named your estate, rather than individuals, as beneficiary to your retirement plans? If you have, you have accidentally accelerated your tax liability when you die.

### Management Issues

Does management interact regularly with employees and make them feel like part of the success of your business? Are your employees coached to fix a problem when they make a mistake?

Have you considered a monthly report of unkept promises to customers, prepared by each office or location? This will help focus everyone on attentive customer service and taking care of your customers' needs in a timely fashion.

## Organizational Issues

Is there a process in place to fully evaluate how new ideas for the growth of your business are implemented? Here is a samle list of questions you might ask:

Is the idea financially viable?

Is there a strategy for the allocation of resources?

Do you have personnel with proper skills available to increase the sales and deliver the product? If not, is adequate training provided?

Will your focus be pulled from other critical functions?

Will the idea be completed on time and be fully functional?

Are there too many uncompleted projects?

How are employees prioritizing their activities?

Has management helped them establish priorities?

Are goals clearly communicated to the appropriate people?

Is there a system in place to keep management aware of the status of all projects?

How does accountability break down?

Is the idea part of your core business?

Are all people who contribute valuable insight into the evaluation process included in the decision to move forward?

Are contingencies in place to deal with negative results? Do employees understand what your company does?

Do employees understand the rationale for change?

How do you eat an elephant? One bite at a time.

These are only a small sample of the kinds of questions that help uncover opportunities. You'll have many more when you've assessed your financial information, reviewed corporate documents and surveyed your key employees.

How do you eat an elephant? One bite at a time. You can't tackle all the issues at once. Take your top ten into your Profit Super Bowl and ask everyone to take a bite. This is the last step you'll have to perform alone during the Profit Enhancement Process.

Now let's learn how the Profit Enhancement Process shares the responsibility for profit-making.

# Instant Replays

You can't tackle problems unless you know what they are. You can't leap into profit opportunities until you have identified them.

Great profit coaches spend 33% of their time on product service and idea development, 33% on coaching, and 34% on implementing the new Profit Plan.

Never, never, never stop asking questions.

Start your Profit Audit with a profitability tour of your business.

The Profit Audit provides you with a scouting report of profit possibilities—not answers.

Financial statements are the scoreboard from last season. Ask yourself: what should we do better next season?

Ask your employees! They know 70 percent of the answers.

Create a profit opportunities checklist of the issues you've discovered and pick the top ten. These are the first plays your Profit Team should consider practicing.

How do you eat an elephant? One bite at a time.

# Chapter 4

# TEAM PRACTICE:
## Building a Winning Profit Game Team

This was the first seminar where we rose above personalities and finger pointing and focused entirely on the issues. We also brought to the table those "sacred cows," which are always there but no one talks about. We discussed these openly and discovered ways of disposing of all of them.

– Ronald P. Ruchalski, President, East End Moving & Storage, Inc.

Again you wowed us at our recent Profit Enhancement seminar. Thank you.You have brought me back into the flock of the faithful and showed me how good I really have it, not how tough the road is that I walk as a small business CEO. You truly are a friend and I appreciate you, Barry, both as friend and consultant. My Dad told me that it would be lonely at the top, however, with friends like you my loneliness is shared.

–Philip N. Potvin, President, Western Concrete Products Co.

In this chapter you are invited to participate in a profit management retreat. We call it the Profit Super Bowl because it's the time when your top team, your starters, pull together to create the game plan to win. It's the time when your star performers get an opportunity to take the company to the top. Those chosen to participate should be experienced players, trained in the company's strategies and goals, and dedicated to winning.

During the Profit Super Bowl the starting team works together to develop a Profit Plan for your business. They work through a process of discovering previously unrealized profit possibilities and identifying strategies for adding them to the bottom line.

Here, it is everyone's job, as members of your starting

Profit Team, to share ideas that will make the organization more successful. We've already discussed how most employees do work that is functional, but it may not add real value to the company. This session will define activities that will change the way people work—from just completing tasks that satisfy their department's functions to participating in the development of a truly profitable business whose success benefits—and depends upon—everyone in the business.

---

"I can is more important than I.Q."
—Clark A. Johnson, Chairman of the Board, Pier 1

---

In this chapter you will participate in a "virtual" Profit Super Bowl, where you will learn how the responsibility for profit*ability* is shared among management. You'll see managers coming up with great new profit-enhancing ideas because they are really going to begin to understand the bottom line possibilities...the big picture. One good idea will lead to another as they learn that profit achievements are more important than completed tasks. You'll see managers discovering that their job is to identify financial opportunities and be responsible for turning ideas into dollars in addition to their other assignments.

In this chapter we are the outside Profit Advisors who will facilitate the group through various Profit Team building exercises, focusing on improving the organization's bottom line. During this session, managers will discover and identify areas that will make the business more profitable, in total harmony with the goals and objectives of the business. Then they will organize profit project committees that define the company's profit goals, and develop strategies to achieve them.

Soon you'll understand how effective it is for the group to discuss the financial ideas suggested by individual members and how they should be implemented. Together we will set financial goals for each profit project which are specific and measurable, and fix accountability and responsibility for each. We know that without quantifiable financial goals, profits will not occur. What you can measure, you can manage. Profit goals should be motivational. Remember, profit results are the name of the game. Without a map you get lost, or worse, you may never get there at all. Financial goals should be in total harmony with the business's goals and objectives.

The focus of this Profit Super Bowl is to maximize the organization's bottom line. We encourage our clients to focus first on "quick fix" and easily attainable goals that can be realistically attained over a a short period of time. This gives them the confidence necessary to pursue more difficult opportunities later on. The Profit Plan developed during this workshop will inventory resources, labor dollars, and goals and describe how they will be used most effectively to reach the ultimate goals of the company. We believe that business profit planning is really the act of matching available information and resources with educated estimates to project bottom line possibilities.

> Your goal—a Profit Plan that is a bottom line, logical strategy for finding profits in a whole new way.

What exactly is a Profit Plan—as opposed to a budget or business plan? A Profit Plan is a bottom line-oriented, logical strategy. It takes into account literally dozens of ways you are letting money slip through your fingers. It's a shift in corporate culture, implemented by management, but carried out by every employee in your firm. A Profit Plan forces you, and everyone in your organization, to look for profits in a whole new way, and in so many fresh new areas that you'll be amazed at its leverage ability.

Some profit strategies will be obvious. You may already be practicing them to a lesser degree. But the Profit Super Bowl is a time for pulling them out and looking at everything your business does today that it could be doing better, including strategies you haven't tried yet.

The Profit Super Bowl is being held right here in this book. Dress is casual. Your ideas are very important to us. Your attendance is absolutely necessary for the entire session. You may find that one retreat is all you need, but most of our clients find that regularly scheduled Profit Team meetings keep the fires burning year after year.

---

Your guest list should include everyone you think has the best ideas for your company and who will put forth the effort to turn ideas into bottom line results.

---

Just as in those first important scrimmages the team plays before the season begins, you'll want to chose your best players for this management retreat—those who are ready for action.

Every great coach knows you can't win by yourself. So a profit coach can't improve profit*ability* by working in a vacuum. The real reason for holding the Profit Super Bowl is that it's difficult for any one individual to see the whole picture, but everyone can see part of it. The retreat is an opportunity for the starting team—representing each major department—to come together with their own ideas and be prepared to listen to others. The profit retreat shifts the sole burden for making profits from the CEO to a shared responsibility with the Profit Team. It transforms team members into leaders of the profit ideas they generate and teams they develop. So identify and make the guest list carefully. Each is invited to join this group because he or she has the following personal characteristics:

- A thorough understanding of their function in the business;
- The ability to comprehend the big picture, not merely one aspect of it;
- The willingness to search for better ways of doing things;
- The willingness to change;

---

The most expensive cost in a business is the cost of a closed mind.

---

- A passion for helping the company be successful and a high energy level;
- The ability to work effectively with other members of the Profit Team in a peer-group environment;
- The commitment and authority to make the time to devote to profit projects;
- The belief that being selected by the company to serve as a Profit Team member is an honor; and
- A positive profit attitude and commitment to serve as an effective member of the Profit Team.

Each manager will receive an invitation and a challenge similar to the one we've made to you as the profit coach.

---

It's difficult for any one individual to see the whole picture, but everyone can see part of it.

---

Nearly every person who works in a business has ideas, but most businesses have no forum for communicating those ideas. How much effort is spent trying to encourage ideas? For years a major U.S. car manufacturer had problems with the quality of their paint. They hired expensive consultants. No one could help. One day a supervisor went down and asked people in the paint shop if they had ideas to improve the quality of paint on the vehicles. One bright line worker responded to this question with, "Yes, I thought you'd never ask." She had the solution and was glad to share it.

Most organizations have a CEO, a CFO, and even a COO; but how many have"PEOs"? A PEO is a Profit Enhancement Officer, charged with developing and implementing good, new profit ideas. Who should be this PEO? *Everyone* in your organization.

At the start of our profit brainstorming session we'll appoint all the participants as "PEOs" to get them thinking about those ideas. And when it's over you'll want to make everyone in your organization into a PEO, too.

---

Some businesses like to play it too safe. They set the bar for performance too low. But if that bar is raised by the Profit Team, and you are successful as a group, the organization will jump even higher.

---

The Profit Super Bowl must be a nonthreatening forum for sharing ideas. It is also the time to transform management teams that manage the affairs of their department into Profit Teams focused on the bottom line of the company as a whole. Most people in an organization don't know how high to jump. It's never been communicated to them. The Profit Super Bowl allows everyone to realize the potential of the company and their contribution to it. Some businesses like to play it safe, the bar for performance is set too low. If that bar is raised by the Profit Team, and you are successful as a group, the organization will jump even higher. Henry Ford once said, "If you think you can or you think you can't, you're probably right."

---

Expectations create results. You get what you expect—NOT what you want.

---

The Profit Super Bowl delegates the responsibility for improving the bottom line to all Profit Team members. It transforms them into profit leaders for the future. It emphasizes the impact they as individuals have on the bottom line. Team members get excited and accept challenges. That's why this retreat needs the starting team from each department. However, there has to be an attendee limit. Keep the group to 20 or fewer per session. The retreat for a large corporation might involve various divisional Profit Super Bowls that lead to an "All-Star" game with the best from each team invited to attend.

The first Profit Super Bowl should be an "away" game where no one from the home office will interrupt.

We recommend that the CEO appoint a meeting coordinator to make all the arrangements for the Profit Super Bowl. Hold it away from the office. A nearby hotel meeting room is best so that there is complete focus on the meeting without the traditional office interruptions. In the meeting room, tables and chairs should be set up in the shape of a horseshoe to allow all participants to feel equal and to see each other. The room should be equipped with all the audio-visual equipment you feel is necessary.

The meeting coordinator should make sure the room is a comfortable temperature, that there is adequate lighting, and enough space for everyone to work comfortably. The more natural sunlight, the more energy participants will feel.

Each participant should receive updated financial information. If you feel it is necessary, delete selected information you are uncomfortable sharing with the group.

When we facilitate a Profit Super Bowl, we ask the coordinator to arrange for rewards: $250 worth of two dollar bills! Why? Because two dollar bills are unusual. A two dollar bill signifies that unusual dollars are rewarded for unusual ideas and efforts. Award the two-dollar bills, or other rewards as you choose, to participants who provide valuable ideas during the session. On the back of the two-dollar bill is a picture of the Continental Congress working on the Declaration of Independence. Could we say this was America's first Profit Super Bowl?

"People like to be rewarded for their efforts," says Larry Pecattiello, our football coach friend. The Detroit Lions reward their players during the team meeting after each game. "Some of these players are making millions of dollars a year, but you should see how proud they are when we hand them a $100 bill in front of their peers. We give a $100 bill to the player who made the best sack, the best hit, the most decisive third down; and we reward the guy who tried hardest."

Coaching is motivating team members to try harder. Larry never criticizes a player for a bad move in front of the rest of the team. "If you want to motivate someone," he says, "only motivate in a praiseworthy way in front of his peers."

At the beginning of the meeting, appoint one person as note taker, responsible for capturing all agreed-upon profit strategies. This person is the football team's equivalent of the team statistician. Be sure to emphasize how important this job is. When we facilitate the Profit Super Bowl, we provide a specially formatted Excel spreadsheet for the "team statistician" to record ideas and assignments for each profit project.

---

The Profit Super Bowl is played strictly by the rules. Strict guidelines ensure that the Profit Plan will emerge strong, focused, and with motivating concensus.

---

The Profit Super Bowl is a nonthreatening forum, an opportunity to talk about the tough issues in a friendly way.

No one should get personal. We encourage talk about issues, not people. We challenge participants to discuss what can work—not what hasn't.

The rules for the Profit Super Bowl must be as follows:

1. *Listen with attention.*

2. *Stay focused with intention.*

3. *No sacred cows. Say what needs to be said. Speak the unspeakable.*

4. *Don't attack people. Attack business concepts.*

5. *No "cheap shots."*

6. *Respect differences of opinion rather than placing the blame.*

7. *Focus on solving problems.*

8. *Only new information will be discussed.*

9. *Keep it positive. Help others develop their ideas. No negative statements are allowed at this meeting. Thus none of the following foul language:*
   *"Don't be ridiculous."*
   *"Let's shelve it for right now."*
   *"We're not ready for that."*
   *"It won't work here."*
   *"Our business is different."*
   *"Let's think about it some more."*
   *"We did all right without it."*
   *"It's too radical a change."*
   *"Management won't like it."*
   *"Where did you dig up that idea?"*
   *"It's not practical."*
   *"We've never done it before."*
   *"I have something better."*
   *"It's too risky."*
   *"Let's be sensible."*
   *"We can't afford that."*
   *"We'll never get it approved."*
   *"It's good, but. . ."*
   *"Let's check on it later."*
   *"Too much work."*
   *"Let's get back to reality."*
   *"That's been tried before."*
   *"You can't be serious."*

*These are the kinds of remarks that hold back any discussion, but particularly our nonthreatening forum where ideas are supposed to flow freely. Keep it positive!*

*10. Only one discussion at a time.*

*11. Look at your business through the eyes of a Profit Enhancement Officer.*

*12. Represent the company, not your department or function.*

You as profit coach are not exempt from the rules. You are a participant, too, not the big boss. You retain the veto power, but are urged to use it sparingly. In fact, the less the CEO says and the more he or she listens, the more successful the retreat. A client once informed us that God gave us two ears and one mouth so that we can listen twice as much as we talk. This should be your rule for the Profit Super Bowl, and the words you do speak should be of encouragement, support, acknowledgment, and recognition.

Keep the group on target for achieving the goals of the retreat. Keep pushing for action when the discussion gets bogged down. Move the agenda when appropriate. Monitor the rules and provide a framework for each issue, broadening it when it seems to represent a larger issue than is generally perceived by members of the Profit Team. When and if they get personal, focus on what's good for the company and keep the human element out of the discussions.

---

In too many businesses, profit happens randomly. The employees are like players playing without a scoreboard. They need to know if they are winning or losing to be effective team players in the Profit Game.

---

You're all gathered around the room, comfortable and eager to begin. Your first goal is to transform this room full of managers and employees into a Profit Team.

Start with a PEP talk. Tell the group why you are gathered and what your expectations are for this particular session and for the process as a whole. Use this opportunity to inspire your team. Suggest that rewards may be offered in the future—both cash and non-cash—for coming up with new ideas, when they add value to the company's bottom line. Describe how they will be rewarded for putting forth the effort to turn those ideas into bottom line results. If the company is more successful, those who make it happen will be also.

Then ask the group to identify their goals for the session and write these on a flip chart. As an example, one of our clients, a firm of professionals, offered these expectations:

1. Create new ways for increasing the inventory of services we have to offer clients at higher billing rates;
2. Provide the groundwork for billing 20 percent additional revenues over the next 12 months;
3. Change the culture to make the practice more fun and more profitable;
4. Open lines of communication;
5. Come up with a plan for profit project implementation;
6. Create greater perception of value to our clients for services which will generate more profit for the firm;
7. Increase client satisfaction with the firm;
8. Gain new outlook on client relationships;
9. Feel better about what we do with our own careers because of the way clients feel about our firm;
10. Promote teamwork in our firm by sharing client projects.

This list is displayed during the entire Profit Super Bowl, so that you and your group will be reminded of your goals.

---

Begin the Profit Game by transforming your managers into a powerhouse Profit Team. Then make everyone in the organization a PEO (Profit Enhancement Officer).

---

Now you must get your team ready to play—to change the way they think, view the world, and act. Unlike traditional management teams, you want your group to feel a greater degree of ownership and commitment to financially quantified profit projects.

- Management teams advance the cause of their department, while Profit Teams advance the cause of their organization's bottom line.
- Managers focus on yesterday. Profit Team members focus on tomorrow.
- Managers accept responsibility for the business issues associated with their department.
- Profit Teams identify financial strategies that enhance the bottom line of the organization, designate Profit Champions to be responsible for each profit project, establish quantifiable financial goals, set meaningful completion dates and determine their relative importance, and are responsible for turning profit ideas into bottom line results.

We find that once people develop profit*ability,* they alter their viewpoint and realize the possibilities open to them as they help the business become more profitable, excitement glows and commitment grows. The immediate challenge is to transmit this excitement not only to this all-important starting team but throughout the organization. The breakthrough occurs when this diverse group of people work together to create a Profit Plan with identified strategies they agree are vital, then carry their enthusiasm back to the rest of the team. Once the paradigm has shifted, ideas flow.

---

Assign each player a "position," a role in your emerging Profit Plan.

---

Now that each participant's focus is profit, how are they going to help generate it? We go around the room asking each person such questions as:

- Describe the company's profit strategy.
- Justify why you have a job with this firm.
- Describe the connection between the work you do and how it benefits the bottom line.
- What are your primary responsibilities?
- How is what you are doing today going to make the company more successful in the future?

Openly discuss each participant's role in the company. Often other participants will add comments about what that person has said about his or her job because they contribute to the company in ways that they don't recognize themselves. This helps the group understand the basic responsibilities of everyone and appreciate their place in the organization.

At the end of this discussion we praise anyone who mentioned the essentials of successful businesses:

- Profit generation so that the company has more choices and options available.
- Fulfilling the mission/vision of the company.
- Providing world-class customer service for customers.

Your organization must have PRIDE (Personal Responsibility In Delivering Excellence).

As we know from previous chapters, it's rare for an employee to link his or her job into the bigger picture. So here you can begin to explore the company's mission and vision and relate each person's job and responsibility for adding value to it. The goals of Profit Teams are defined as enhancing profit*ability* while providing "world-class customer service" (doing things so well that whomever you do it for, asks for more) and accomplishing the mission of the business, getting there because of a vision. A great quarterback's "mission" is to beat the other team; his "vision" is to throw the ball to where he thinks the receiver will be. In football you need a well-balanced team composed of offense, defense and special teams. In business, there must be a balance among profit, world-class service, and mission/vision to have a profit*able*, well-run company. Further, the business must achieve the goal of satisfied long-term employees. You can't have the first three without this fourth element.

---

Define your goal: To have everyone in the organization working towards realizing its bottom line potential, in harmony with the company's strategic goals and objectives.

---

This leads naturally into an introduction of the concept of unrealized bottom line potential. You can't realize your bottom line potential unless you discover your unrealized profit potential. Focus on the five engines that drive a successful business:

<u>The Five Engines that Drive A Successful Business</u>

Employees
Organizational Structure
Sales and Marketing
Operations
Financial Management

As you focus on each of these five areas, tell the team what was uncovered in that area through the employee and customer surveys and the Profit Audit. Show the group how the company was ranked in these five areas. Show them on the scale of 1 to 10 the potential for profit that exists between the way the company operates today and what could be achieved in the future. Our experience is that most businesses fall below six in two to five of the engine categories, leaving 40 percent of the capacity unutilized. How effective is a team operating at 60 percent of profit capacity? Once the starting team accepts the fact that there is substantial unrealized profit for them to go after, they'll begin to examine the essential aspects, ideas, and processes of the organization with growing enthusiasm.

---

Before the group recognizes new profit strategies, they have to deal with the challenges. What is preventing the organization from achieving its full profit potential?

---

A great football coach can tell you what caused the "fumbles" in each important game. You've performed your Profit Audit and now know what's causing those "profit fumbles" in your business. Help your team identify these profit fumbles as well as their causes. Ask what is holding the company back financially, and what each manager can be doing that he or she is not doing today to realize more profits for the company? Let employees know it's their job to add value to the bottom line. Involve them in identifying profit strategies, so those profit fumbles won't keep the company from making that all-important third down. Explore how profit fumbles have a negative effect on the final score. Profit equals income minus expenses including those profit fumbles. They are similar to sales returns—you earned it, and now you have to give it back. They minimize the bottom line. Profit is what's left at the end of the day. Have the group identify the profit fumbles that are keeping your business from winning and beating your competition.

---

Profit fumbles are really opportunities to score in disguise.

---

Now introduce some of your priority profit opportunity issues for general discussion. Help your team discover them for themselves.

For instance, if you identified sales and marketing as a weak area, have the group discuss ways to increase sales for the company:

- Increase the number of customers,
- Sell more to each customer, and
- Increase the value of each sales transaction.

Pricing is another important issue identified in most Profit Audits. The selling price of goods and services is perhaps one of the most central business decisions an organization must make. Profits begin with the sale, in concert with the proper selling price. If products and services are not priced effectively, profits will be sacrificed needlessly. Focus on pricing strategies that fit into your customer profiles.

---

Introduce your Profit Team to the way to play and win the game—The Profit Enhancement Process.

---

The Profit Enhancement Process is in no way just cutting expenses. No business can cost-cut its way to prosperity. The key to financial success involves creating a profit culture along with effective cost controls and innovative ways of increasing sales and profit margins. Generating profits requires a process just like every other normal business activity.

As members of the Profit Team, the group is charged with:

- Sharing responsibility for profitability;
- Establishing financial strategies that will improve profitability;
- Setting meaningful, measurable financial goals
- Fixing accountability so that certain people are responsible for getting each profit project accomplished;

- Implementing and coordinating profit activities so that profitable ideas turn into financial successes.

Imagine the power of this starting team when it begins working closely with the soon-to-be-appointed Profit Activity Leader (PAL) to carry out the new profit initiatives defined during your Profit Super Bowl! You will be there to support their efforts with extra resources and time to ensure that the profit projects stay on track. You will see to it that their activities will be measured, monitored, and nurtured towards enhanced financial results.

Profit Teams implement change most effectively. Properly coached, they make informed bottom line improvement decisions, rather than just decisions. They are closer to the reality of what's going on in the organization than owners, because of their personal involvement and experiences. Coaching the implementation of profit projects is as important as deciding which activities should be tackled to begin with. Profit Teams take ownership of financial opportunities because they are part of the process that identifies them. Thus, they willingly accept responsibility for implementation. Proactivitity is foremost on their agenda.

Profit Teams do much more than just manage rank-and-file employees. Typically, managers accept responsibility for the business issues associated with their department. Profit Teams identify financial strategies that enhance the bottom line of their organization in harmony with strategic goals and objectives, designate Profit Champions to be responsible for each profit project, establish quantifiable financial goals, set meaningful completion dates and are responsible for turning profit ideas into bottom line results.

---

Put your Profit Team onto the field to practice their new plays, and let the good ideas flow.

---

The Profit Team is now ready to practice their own ideas for improving the company's bottom line. Break the Profit Team down into smaller groups, each charged with developing five profit-enhancing strategies.

Each idea must be completed with:

- Action date—when will the business begin to realize a financial benefit;
- Profit Champion—the individual responsible for managing the project;
- Degree of Difficulty—whether the project has a high, low, or medium degree of difficulty to accomplish it;
- Priority—how important is the idea—whether the project has a high, medium or low priority;
- Unrealized bottom line potential—quantified in dollars;
- Realized bottom line potential—filled in later as the actual financial results are achieved;
- Financial assumptions—notes on how unrealized bottom potential was computed.

This is the first real quantification of the value the project will add to the company's bottom line. It must be based on an educated estimate of gross income less related expenses. For example, if the profit idea increases sales, estimate the additional profit margin on one sale. Multiply that amount by the projected number of units that will be sold to determine the gross profit. Then subtract additional expenses incurred as a result of the idea. The goal is to determine the realistic bottom line potential for each profit project that has yet to be realized—the unrealized bottom line potential.

---

Turn short-yardage plays into big gains.

---

As head profit coach, meet briefly with each group. Remember, you are the only one who knows your top profit priorities. Make sure that each of these priorities becomes a profit strategy in at least one of the Profit Team huddles. Never insist that the group implement it; just ask if they believe it to be a worthy project, and see if they take it from there. Also expand each suggested issue so that it becomes a bigger one, more global than local. For instance, someone may suggest that customer service operators are sometimes rude to customers. Your job as coach is to help the team discover why. Are customer service operators overworked? Do they know everything about the products so they don't have to run around asking other busy people questions? Are they properly trained? Are certain issues that affect one department more global than the group realizes? Do they actually affect various other departments as well?

---

The real power of the Profit Super Bowl is the creation of a culture that brings employees into the profit process and assists them in taking ownership of profit strategies that enhance the bottom line.

---

Without profit coaching, your starting team will never get to the Profit Super Bowl. Help your team generate ideas. Broaden them, and expand your starters' perspectives.

---

Select plays from your new playbook and turn them into a full-blown game plan. Put the Profit Plan together.

---

Once the groups have formulated their ideas, gather again to discuss them as a group. Start recording profit strategies on large sheets of paper taped around the room so everyone can watch the plan unfold. We have created attention-grabbing software templates which systematically record the Profit Plan. It is projected, using an LCD, for the group to observe. It is exhilarating for the team to see their ideas entered into our software, with the focus on the dollars of unrealized bottom line potential each profit project will generate. Without this software, be sure you record the following:

1. Each profit project idea
2. Its action date
3. Who is responsible for its implementation
4. Whose idea it is
5. Degree of difficulty
6. Priority (the relative importance of the issue to your company)
7. Quantified, unrealized bottom line potential in dollars
8. Financial assumptions used to determine the unrealized bottom line potential

The Profit Advisors' proprietary software template actually adds up the unrealized bottom line potential so that after each profit idea and at the end of the session, the group looks with amazement at the possibility dollars they have discovered. A Profit Champion (or project leader) for each strategy should be selected along with profit project committee members. After the Profit Super Bowl, each responsible manager, or Profit Champion, will select a committee, if needed, from the rest of the company's employees to carry out their profit initiative. They will then lay out the process to turn the idea into financial results.

- Each profit strategy requires identifying, step-by-step and task-by-task, what is required to accomplish it. Remember, there is only one way to eat an elephant, one bite at a time. The goal is to break a big idea into comprehensible and manageable tasks.

■ Review with attention and intention the financial assumptions for each strategy. If the idea is successfully carried out, what will it contribute to the bottom line? It is critical that these estimates be extremely conservative so that expectations will be met with realistic support and be credible. The goal is to under-promise and over-deliver. Later, the Profit Teams will define additional tasks as they develop their own project.

■ The "Action Date" is when the company will begin to benefit financially from each strategy. This is the date when all preparations are completed and you are ready to begin playing the Profit Game. After the retreat, additional dates will be assigned for each specific task.

■ To keep enthusiasm high and good ideas flowing, give out the two-dollar bills or other rewards to every person who originated a profit-generating idea, as well as to those Profit Champions who will be carrying them out. The starting team congratulates one another for each strategy with growing gusto, and begins to compete for additional rewards themselves. This is what you want to continue happening in a more meaningful way when you get back to day-to-day reality. During the Profit Super Bowl, each special team offers its most significant issues. Often there is overlap, but you as profit coach can encourage each team to suggest at least one profit strategy, and be rewarded for it.

■ Most importantly, there must be a consensus that to tackle an idea, if accepted, will be for the good of the organization. Remember, you have veto authority at this point ("the man with the gold, rules"). Our experience is that this is rarely done. You'll wind up with a profit fumble if you do.

- Make sure each strategy is thoroughly reviewed and analyzed, depending upon its significance to the company. Our Detroit Lions coach and friend, Larry Pecattiello, says players are presented with each new play verbally, visually through films of past games, and in a written form. Then they practice it. This way team members have an opportunity to hear it, see it, then practice it.

Let's look at the worksheet (opposite page) we use to help clients manage their Profit Plan. The following is a sample Profit Project Worksheet for a Profit Plan which we create on our template as we coach the client's starting team.(Names and dates have been changed.)

Once information is agreed upon by the Profit Team and recorded in the worksheet, only negotiations between each Profit Champion and the Profit Activities Leader will alter it.

At the end of the session, add up all the unrealized bottom line potential, and voila! The Profit Plan—complete with strategies, accountability, financial measures, and supporting information—is ready to put into action.

To sum up our session, the group now reviews the list of expectations they developed at the beginning of the Profit Super Bowl. We review each item to ensure expectations have been exceeded. They always are, because the Profit Team is proudly part of the process.

As a concluding exercise, each member of the Profit Team summarizes their commitment and evaluates the benefits of the retreat. We ask them to look at this exercise from the following three perspectives:

- Themselves (the participant)
- The group (the Profit Team as an entity)
- The company (the organization)

## A Profit-Focused Company's Profit Plan-Project Worksheet

| Profit Project | Action date | Profit Plan Champion | Profit Plan Idea Generator | Priority (1 high 2 med 3 low) | Degree of Difficulty (1 high 2 med 3 low) | Unrealized Bottom Line Potential** | Realized Bottom Line Profit* |
|---|---|---|---|---|---|---|---|
| 1- Maximize delivery loads from factory to stores. | 1/1/99 | Joe | Sam | 2 | 3 | $100,000 | |
| 2 - Improve sales process in the followng areas: Incoming telephone inquiries, Cross-selling, Developing sales database | 2/1/00 | Carl | Webb | 1 | 2 | $565,000 | |
| 3 - Establish acceptable moisture contents for raw materials. | 2/1/99 | Larry | Laura | 2 | 1 | $100,000 | |
| 4 - Repair broken pallets rather than buy new ones, & evaluate their size in relationship to what they hold. | 2/1/99 | Ray | Chuck | 2 | 3 | $ 80,000 | |
| 5 - Recycle shipping materials that are used on incoming deliveries. | 2/1/99 | Sue | Curtis | 3 | 3 | $18,000 | |
| 6 - Determine the causes of manufacturing products that do not meet our quality standards. Establish a process to minimize the cost of waste in production by not doing things right the first time. | 2/1/00 | Bruce | David | 1 | 1 | $220,000 | |
| 7 - Establish a close-out procedure for excess inventory. | 6/1/99 | Dina | Allan | 2 | 3 | $180,000 | |
| 8 - Develop and implement a preventative maintenance plan for equipment, so that the manufacturing process doesn't stop when machinery breaks down. | 1/1/00 | Steve | Todd | 1 | 2 | $259,00 | |
| | | | | | **Totals** | **$1,522,000** | * |

**The "realized" column will not be completed until results have occurred.*

*** The financial assumptions used to quantify the unrealized bottom line potential are recorded on other worksheets for subsequent review.*

Most of these evaluations are very positive. After a Profit Super Bowl coached by one of our Florida members of the Institute of Profit Advisors, a participant praised:

> The Enhancement program helped me make the decision to stay. . . even though yesterday I received an unsolicited employment opportunity with another company, with a larger salary; 100% paid health insurance; 4 weeks paid vacation; 4 weeks paid sick leave, hours of 6:30 a.m. to 2:30 p.m. I believe in the goals of this seminar and decided I would much prefer to be a part of the team implementing these programs.

Other successful Profit Super Bowls we've facilitated have elicited such glowing participant remarks as:

> "From your initial presentation of the Profit Enhancement Process, I was captivated by the idea, and excited by the potential for both increased profitability and enhanced teamwork; now, upon completion of the entire process, I remain captivated and excited."

▪

> "I increased my overall knowledge of the company…I am beginning to experience the feeling of belonging and not as an outsider."

▪

> "I'm refocused, renewed and have further built my belief that this company can and will be even more successful. Energized. It helped me see some of the problems others are having as well as the incredible opportunities."

▪

> "My pledge for the next 21 days will be to make a commitment to excellence every day."

During the Profit Game—always monitor progress, cheer along the sidelines, and consult with assistant coaches and players.

Finally, review the implementation system that is discussed in the next chapter. Each Profit Champion completes a report of how they will implement their profit project. It is vital that the Profit Activities Leader continue the enthusiasm, excitement and momentum that was created by the Super Bowl.

The day after a banking client's Profit Super Bowl that we facilitated with a Pennsylvania member of the Institute of Profit Advisors, we met with the Profit Champions to discuss their implementation plans. One Champion came in weeping. Her immediate boss had already tried to force her to fumble her profit project. He had participated in the Profit Super Bowl, and agreed to accept her profit project then. Why was he being so uncooperative now? We talked with the president of the bank and urged him to prevent a profit fumble before the profit project could roll away. The president was determined that the Profit Enhancement Process succeed. He gave our Profit Champion's supervisor a choice: either do what the Profit Team had agreed upon during the Profit Super Bowl, or leave the company. The choice wasn't pleasant for him. It showed the president was committed. The profit fumble was recovered and the supervisor began applauding the employee's work on her profit project!

# Instant Replays

"I can is more important than I.Q."
—Clark A. Johnson, Chairman of the Board, Pier 1

Your goal—a profit plan that is a bottom line, logical strategy for finding profits in a whole new way.

Your guest list should include everyone you think has the best ideas for your company and who will put forth the effort to turn ideas into bottom line results.

The most expensive cost in a business is the cost of a closed mind.

It's difficult for any one individual to see the whole picture, but everyone can see part of it.

Some businesses like to play it too safe. They set the bar for performance too low. But if that bar is raised by the Profit Team, and you are successful as a group, the organization will jump even higher.

Expectations create results. You get what you expect —NOT what you want.

The first Profit Game should be an "away" game where no one from the home office will interrupt.

The Profit Super Bowl is played strictly by the rules. Strict guidelines ensure that the Profit Plan will emerge strong, focused, and with motivating concensus.

In too many businesses, profit happens randomly. The employees are like players playing without a scoreboard. They need to know if they are winning or losing to be effective team players in the Profit Game.

Begin the Profit Game by transforming your managers into a powerhouse Profit Team. Then make everyone in the organization a PEO (Profit Enhancement Officer).

Assign each player a "position," a role in your emerging Profit Plan.

Define your goal: To have everyone in the organization working towards realizing its bottom line potential, in harmony with the company's strategic goals and objectives.

Before the group recognizes new profit strategies, they have to deal with the challenges. What is preventing the organization from achieving its full profit potential?

Profit fumbles are really opportunities to score in disguise.

Introduce your Profit Team to the way to play and win the game—The Profit Enhancement Process.

Put your Profit Team onto the field to practice their new plays, and let the good ideas flow.

Turn short-yardage plays into big gains.

The real power of the Profit Super Bowl is the creation of a culture that brings employees into the profit process and assists them in taking ownership of profit strategies that enhance the bottom line.

Select plays from your new playbook and turn them into a full-blown game plan. Put the Profit Plan together.

During the Profit Game—always monitor progress, cheer along the sidelines, and consult assistant coaches and players.

# Chapter 5

# WINNING THE SUPER BOWL
## Implementing Your Profit Plan

We currently have between 6 and 10 projects underway; each being managed by separate teams, each with its own unique profit opportunity. At the same time we have already implemented some of our programs and are beginning to enjoy returns from the energy and the initiatives that you helped us create.

–Barry P. Foreman, President, CEO, Forman Brothers Inc.

I must tell you that, while the workshop itself was worth the investment many times over, some of the most exciting times in our organization have come from helping the management staff achieve their ways and tasks.

–Michael C. Martin, President, Dudley Martin Chevrolet

---

The more you get people to write down their commitments, the better chance you will have to win the Profit Game.

---

Implementation is the most important step in the entire Profit Enhancement Process. It is where the rubber hits the road because effective implementation means good ideas go somewhere—to your bottom line.

The implementation process *is* the Super Bowl of business—the time when your profit teams really show their worth and score—right to your bottom line. The more you encourage people to write down their commitments, the better chance you will have for profit success. Expectations create results.

So before we even begin this chapter, read and sign this pledge. (We want to make sure you are convinced and commited.)

## The CEO's Pledge

Profit is a journey that never ends. It is the result of a series of small steps that, added together, will dramatically improve the performance of our company. Our company has been in business for ___ years. Practices which have been in effect for years cannot be changed overnight. I recognize that there are no quick fixes in this world. Improvements to our bottom line will take time and hard work. I understand that the following rules will hasten profit improvement for our firm. Also, I recognize that their violation will handicap the realization of our profit goals.

As part of our Profit Enhancement Process, an inventory of profit initiatives will be identified and a commitment made to successfully implement them. Profit Teams will be created to work on these projects. Each profit project will have one employee who is responsible for its implementation. There will be specific time designated for completion of each project. The unrealized bottom line potential for each profit project will be computed.

I agree to follow these rules to ensure the success of our Profit Enhancement Process:

1. If a person on the profit project team is not capable or unwilling to do the necessary work, they will be replaced with another employee. For each project team, one person will be designated as Profit Champion, and they will be responsible for implementation.

2. Consequences will be established for non-completion of a profit project.

3. As additional profits are earned, rewards will be provided to Profit Team members whose efforts contribute to our company's success.

4. I will communicate the importance of completing profit projects. I expect Profit Team members to regularly allocate a portion of their work week to the profit projects they are responsible for. The Project Champions will report their progress regularly. I recognize that normal daily interruptions will occur, but I will not accept continued excuses that people are too busy.

5. Initially, the goals of each project will be clearly defined. When the projects are assigned, each Project Champion will prepare an outline of their activities within one week.

6. The ability to obtain "buy in" by members of my management team and employees who are affected by projects will ensure successful implementation.

7. Benchmarks will be set for each project in order to gauge success.

8. I understand that the completion of project tasks will not necessarily lead to immediate profit. It may take months for the results to be realized.

9. I will continually communicate the importance of incorporating a profit culture in my company and stress the sense of urgency to completing the assigned profit-generating tasks.

10. Some projects may require the investment of resources. These requests will be fairly evaluated and quickly resolved.

11. I will continue the quest for profit improvement by encouraging my team to identify and implement additional profit-generating initiatives.

12. When a project is completed, we will institutionalize the required ongoing activities to ensure the realization of the desired profits. As our company embarks on the Profit Enhancement Process, I understand that successful implementation is contingent upon these rules being followed.

---

[To be signed by CEO]

▪

Are you ready to sign this pledge? Then let's go on!

After a Profit Super Bowl, your Profit Team members will be all fired up and ready to begin work on their profit ideas. By the end of the session, the group will have completed the following steps:

- Prioritized profit projects
- Assigned accountability for each task
- Clearly defined profit projects and the steps needed to complete them
- Assigned accountability for each sub-task
- Established benchmarks and measurement processes
- Defined time limits and completion commitments for each task.

Now, let's examine how to control the energy that has been let loose.

---

Project implementation is the key component of maximizing profit.

---

We have all seen this scenario occur: a great idea develops, and everyone agrees that it would be worthwhile for the organization. Enthusiastically, people want to start to make it happen, but over time the project just withers and dies. Why does this happen?

Project implementation is a key component of maximizing corporate profit in the Profit Enhancement Process. We don't believe in starting something we can't finish, and we don't let our clients do so either.

To win the game, a successful football team executes a number of specific activities—the right combination of running, blocking, passing, receiving, tackling, and kicking. They complete their downs, execute punts and kick-offs effectively, and then score more touchdowns than the opponents. What happens when a team is not having a winning season? The coaches help players refocus on the fundamentals of the game, and adopt and adapt to new ideas, plans, plays and processes.

In business, the fundamentals of success are sales and marketing, organizational structure, people, operations and financial management. When your company lags behind in any one of these areas, new ideas must be generated to take care of the short fall. We've seen how the Profit Enhancement Process provides a forum for generating these new ideas, for capturing hidden profit strategies from your starting team, and creates a structure to turn them into completed tasks with measurable financial benefits. We've learned the plays, we've done some practicing during the Profit Super Bowl, and now we are ready to play the Profit Game.

We're out on the field, the fans are cheering in the stands, the referee tosses the coin. Then reality sets in. People get back to their offices and face the pile of work awaiting them. You must focus on possible obstacles first, before they do, to be sure these "reasons" do not destroy your implementation process. You are the master implementer.

Here is a list of typical "reasons" that prevent profit projects from succeeding.

- Pressing daily issues
- People are not sold on the idea
- No buy-in from top management
- Too many issues to deal with
- Project is not clearly defined

- New obstacles arise
- Issue is too big for allocated solution resources
- Lack of consistent motivation
- No clear-cut demonstrable reward system
- Poor communication channels
- Issue develops in another department's domain
- Lack of necessary skills
- Environmental changes occur
- No sense of urgency from participants because target dates weren't set
- No system was established for measuring results
- Unrealistic expectations were set for results
- No consequences were set for failure to accomplish an initiative.

These are big road blocks to success. As profit coach, you've pledged not to let these kinds of fumbles interfere with your Super Bowl win. Now it is your job as profit coach to help your Profit Team Champions and their committees overcome these challenges.

---

Clearly define each project and the steps needed to complete it.

---

During the Profit Super Bowl, the starting team was encouraged to clearly define each issue and pertinent variables by discussing how each profit project might be completed. Profit Champions for every project were selected and the group was committed to it.

This is a good beginning, but let's face it, no matter how important they are when profit projects compete with daily responsibilities, require more financial and/or human resources than originally committed, or need assistance from individuals who are not completely sold on the idea, implementation could be derailed or at least delayed.

To prevent this from happening, consider incorporating the following thoughts into your implementation plan:

- All of the people who will be affected by the idea and are instrumental in its success or failure must be brought in at the beginning.

- There must be an uncompromising and clear-cut commitment from the top that change is good for the organization. There must be a commitment behind the completion of profit projects that allows the appropriate staff to have time to work on their projects. In some cases, this might require that existing duties be prioritized and those of lesser importance delegated, postponed or eliminated.

- Finally, you must inform the entire organization that there is one individual who has the authority to be the "overall champion" for all profit ideas that are in the works. This is the Profit Activities Leader (we call him or her a PAL) who was selected at the Profit Super Bowl. This responsible and respected person provides regular assistance, encouragement and a focal point of accountability for the Profit Team Champions charged with each project. In a nutshell, the PAL's job is to make the Profit Teams successful. He or she is your assistant coach.

---

Every Profit Champion needs support and the opportunity to consult with their PAL.

---

In our system, no one stands alone. Profit project leaders regularly meet with the PAL to review their profit projects. Together they may revise the projects and devise new strategies or in some cases even scrap a project altogether. You can become the PAL if your company is small enough, but in most cases it is the next in charge, perhaps your COO, Executive Vice President or General Manager. Whomever you appoint, it is vital that you hold him or her responsible for the successful implementation of the various profit projects and grant the authority to carry them out.

At the beginning of the implementation process, meet with your Profit Activities Leader and consider the following:

1. Among the profit projects included in the Profit Plan, which are the most important? Alter any you think were incorrectly prioritized.

2. Do you have the right person assigned as Profit Champion for each profit project? Have the best team members been selected for each project?

3. Are the issues and initiatives clearly defined and are they understood?

4. What are the obstacles, from an organizational perspective, that you anticipate?

5. What will be accomplished at your meetings with Project Champions?

6. How will momentum be maintained?

7. What will be the short-and long-term rewards?

When you have determined the answers to these questions, the PAL will be ready to begin meeting regularly with Profit Champions.

As profit coach you'll want to meet frequently with your PAL to assess progress, consult, and act as the reality check to keep the entire process on track.

When you've got this system in place, other causes of profit project breakdown are resolvable. Without this support, it is very difficult, if not impossible, to achieve the hundreds of thousands of dollars envisioned during the Profit Super Bowl.

---

Each Profit Team is responsible for planning their own profit project.

---

Profit project Champions are the next in the chain of command. Your PAL should help them get started with their planning. Each Champion should write a short paragraph describing their vision for their project and what they will accomplish. Then they should list the assumptions the starting team made in adding this project to the Profit Plan, listing the benefits they want to achieve and the obstacles they will face.

We recommend breaking each project into sub-tasks. Remember the adage about eating the elephant one bite at a time. Profit Champions should assign deadlines for each task. Next they should make an initial to-do list for the first task. Then they are ready to meet with their profit project committees.

---

No one, no matter how capable, will be able to implement profit strategies without the help of others in the organization.

---

Profit Teams must work together to implement profit strategies. No one, no matter how capable, will be able to implement profit strategies without the help of others in their organization. To begin the implementation process, each Profit Team should be assembled with their Champion and begin brainstorming how they will develop their project. We created the following acronym to help Profit Teams think through what process is necessary to accomplish their assignments.

**I is for IDENTIFY THE STUMBLING BLOCKS.**
What are the problems you are likely to encounter?

**M is for MANAGE AND MOTIVATE.**
How can you manage this profit project and motivate others to buy into it?

**P is for PLAN.**
Lay out the "big picture" so that others understand just what's involved. Develop a plan to make the ideas happen—one step, one task at a time. Also, work on alternative plans if the original strategy isn't going as planned.

**L is for LEARN.**
Gather information necessary to ensure success. Seek out every source possible. Libraries and books (of course), consultants, the Internet, professional and trade associations, and seminars are just a few sources that will help you learn.

**E is for EXPERIMENT.**
Test your plan, step by step. Don't change everything at one time unless you are satisfied things are working to your satisfaction.

**M is for MEASURE RESULTS.**
If you can't measure the results, you won't really know if your project will improve profitability. What are you going to measure? What benchmarks must be developed to ascertain if progress is being realized?

**E is for EXPEDITE.**
If your experiment is successful, what can be done to expedite this strategy so that profit benefits are accelerated?

**N is for NEEDS.**
Perform a needs analysis to make sure you have the people, technology, know-how, and capital to make this profit strategy successful.

**T is for TENACITY.**
How tenacious is your Profit Team going to be in turning this profit strategy into bottom line results? What commitment is going to be expected?

---

Each team should build a consensus on how they want to work and what they plan to do, step by step, task by task.

---

Brainstorming about each of these items, as it relates to their profit project, helps everyone understand and develop the necessary steps to follow in the process to accomplish it.

Each team should build a consensus on how they want to work and what they plan to do, step by step, task by task. This plan should be formalized by putting it into writing and distributing it to each Profit Champion and to the PAL. It becomes a map as well as a benchmark for progress. Make sure that all the Profit Champions are aware of potential profit fumbles. These could upset their carefully laid out plan, unless they address such concerns in the plan itself. During the PAL's meetings with Champions, the plan is reviewed, progress noted, subsequent deadlines defined, and a summary report prepared for the profit coach each month.

---

Motivate your Profit Teams with a well-touted and fully-understood reward program.

---

Just as the starting team enjoyed the two-dollar bill rewards during their retreat, and the Detroit Lions are often motivated by $100 bills after each game, your employees must know what rewards they can expect from successful completion of their projects. When all employees of a company participate in the Profit Enhancement Process, they are each making a personal investment in the business — of their time, talents, and experience. They each then deserve a portion of the profits their hard work generates (cash and non-cash rewards, including, most importantly, acknowledgment and appreciation).

You and your PAL must make everyone aware that increased profits benefit the entire company. When Profit Champions and their teams prove successful, reward them. If your company has a great year, reward the employees who worked hard to make it happen. If your year wasn't as profit*able* as you expected, do not penalize your employees who tried to increase profits because without them things would have been worse. Reward them. Incentive compensation helps kindle the flames of employee motivation.

Profit Team members and Champions need to be recognized for their efforts. When they effectively perform work which improves the profit*ability* of their organization, they deserve an addition to their bottom line as well. Demonstrating employee appreciation by sharing profits will generate new ideas for profit projects that are never-ending.

And remember, most people don't just work for profit — they work for the benefits that come from profits. Profit provides opportunities and choices. It is the fuel that powers every successful business. That is the real benefit!

---

Bottom up—rather than top down—implementation is the key to winning the Profit Super Bowl.

---

The Profit Enhancement Process trains Profit Teams to become effective problem-solving, opportunity-creating units. Unthinkable ideas are brought up for discussion, discussed in a nonthreatening environment, consensus built, and a plan for implementation enacted. People who are involved "buy into" concepts, add their creative touches and actively work for completion. This is far different than in companies where issues are swept under the rug because they are difficult and cause discomfort. Problems are created in companies when reality is avoided. The best run companies discuss tough topics.

---

Greater profit*ability* comes when players know they are accountable, responsible, and will reap rewards for scoring profits or be penalized if they consistently fail to make it to the profit zone.

---

People do better what is inspected rather than expected. Monitor, evaluate, and acknowledge each task's accomplishment or fumble. PEP provides a well-defined system for implementation.

First, let's pretend you are the Profit Activities Leader. Use the following to guide you as you plan how you will manage the Profit Enhancement Project effectively:

1. Determine the most important projects, and if necessary alter previously established priorities. Doing first things first will propel your project

onto the best course. By now you will have had an opportunity to review the profit projects and, with time, have determined that one or more of them aren't feasible or need to be altered in some way. You may also have seen that some are really more important than their original priority ranking. This is the time to make appropriate alterations to the plan.

2. Do you have the right person assigned as Profit Champion for each project? Do you have the right team members? As head coach, you probably have better insight into how various people work together. You may determine that some of the assigned champions or committees have personality differences or can use a more-qualified Champion. Move with caution and gain consensus to accomplish each project.

3. Review each project and make sure that the issue is clear. This is very important. If the issue is not clear, it will be difficult to establish the steps to achieve it.

4. What are the obstacles, from an organizational perspective, that you anticipate? How are you going to deal with them? Get your strategy in place for each obstacle. Many of these obstacles were brought up at the Profit Super Bowl, but you may discover more and they should be noted at this time.

5. What should you accomplish at the meetings with the Profit Champions? This is your all-important planning function. Understanding the strengths and weaknesses of each Champion as well as each project will help you plan how to effectively manage them. Set agendas for your

meetings. Be open-minded and sensitive, but also firm on the important issues.

6. How will momentum be maintained? What goals, objectives, and deadlines will you set? What incentives will you be able to offer? How will you keep everyone excited and motivated?

7. What will be your short- and long-term rewards? This is a further refinement of number 6.

Now you are ready to begin your meetings with Profit Team Champions. Here is a suggested format for helping each champion focus on his or her project:

**Profit Team Champion's Project Instructions**

1. Write a short paragraph describing the vision of your project and the desired results.

______________________________

______________________________

______________________________

______________________________

______________________________

2. List the assumptions that were made in determining the profit potential of your project.

A.______________________________
B.______________________________
C.______________________________
D.______________________________

3. List the benefits to your company and its employees for pursuing the project.

A.______________________________
B.______________________________
C.______________________________
D.______________________________

4. List project obstacles to overcome. (Obstacles are opportunities in disguise.)

A.____________________________________________

B.____________________________________________

C.____________________________________________

D.____________________________________________

5. List the members of your Profit Team. Note possible causes for assignments to go off track, and record suggestions to stay on track.

| Team Members | Causes for Assignment to Go Off Track | Suggestions for Staying on Track |
|---|---|---|
| | | |
| | | |
| | | |
| | | |
| | | |
| | | |
| | | |

6. What resources will be required to complete your project?

7. How will results be measured?

8. Break the profit project into its most important sub-tasks. Assign a deadline and "Champion" or person in charge of each sub-task.

| | Sub-task | Due date | Champion |
|---|---|---|---|
| A. | | | |
| B. | | | |
| C. | | | |
| D. | | | |

9. Estimate the percentage of completion for the sub-tasks, and assign due dates. (You may also want to establish benchmarks to know that tasks are on target.)

**Sub-task #** **% Completion** **Due Date**

________________________________________

________________________________________

________________________________________

________________________________________

________________________________________

10. Review sub-tasks and list the initial "to-do's." Set deadlines for each. Select Profit Champions for the to-do's. They may be different than the overall Profit Champion.

**Sub-task** **To-Do** **Due Date** **Champion**

A.______________________________________

B.______________________________________

C.______________________________________

D.______________________________________

After your Profit Champions have filled out this form and planned how they will implement their particular project (one bite at a time), set a date and time for your next meeting. At the meeting you will begin to use the following form to monitor progress and establish new goals and deadlines as needed.

**Implementation Coaching Meeting**

Date__________________ Profit Project____________________

Profit Project #_____________________PAL__________________

Team Champion______________________________________

General status since last meeting:
What did you accomplish this week?

________________________________________

________________________________________

________________________________________

________________________________________

________________________________________

What problems did you encounter?

______________________________________________

______________________________________________

______________________________________________

______________________________________________

______________________________________________

Benchmarks met______________________________
Overall % completed___________________________
Negotiated change in completion date: From________To________
**Profit Project Status:**
On track ____ Behind____ Critical___ Abandoned ____
For each existing or new sub-task that had activity this period, specify the following:

| % Completed | Status | Due Date |
|---|---|---|
| | | |
| | | |
| | | |
| | | |

List new "To Do's" that have been created:

| To-Do | Description | Due Date | Priority | Status | Champion |
|---|---|---|---|---|---|
| | | | | | |
| | | | | | |
| | | | | | |
| | | | | | |

Goals to be accomplished by our next meeting:

______________________________________________

______________________________________________

______________________________________________

______________________________________________

Date of next meeting:_____________________________

Addtional suggestions for profit initiatives:

______________________________________________

______________________________________________

______________________________________________

______________________________________________

Profit Champions must be held accountable and know the limits of their authority.

Profit Champions do not have the authority to change their profit projects, action dates, priority codes, or other action items agreed upon during the Profit Super Bowl. In other words, Champions must understand that failing is not an acceptable way to complete what was previously agreed upon. Whether or not the implementation process is proceeding as scheduled, Profit Champions must discuss the progress of their project at their regular meeting with the PAL. If a project is faltering, together they will alter the strategies and find solutions—before it fails.

Profit Champions must receive regular support during implementation. Profit implementation is a group effort with everyone working together to implement the company's Profit Plan.

Winning the Profit Super Bowl will bring hundreds of thousands—even millions—of dollars of previously unrealized profit to your bottom line.

Millions of dollars of profit potential is what it meant to one of our clients, a mega-automobile dealership. As a result of their new profit*ability*, the Profit Team found out that the company was paying the same commission for "hot" car sales as for slower-moving products. They decided it didn't make sense to pay the same commission for easy sales as for harder sells. They devised a new commission structure and brought an additional $360,000 of recurring annual profit to the company's bottom line with this one idea alone.

In addition, the Profit Team discovered that their mechanics had to wait in line at the parts counter to get the work out, sometimes for as long as 45 minutes. The company had planned to hire more mechanics! The Profit Team developed a new system for bringing parts to mechanics, keeping them doing what they should be doing—servicing cars. This new procedure brought in an extra $225,000 in profit potential.

A new utility savings procedure was put in place. Lights and power was minimized during off hours. This simple new procedure saved the company 35 percent on utility bills and brought $50,000 in profit potential to the bottom line.

Keys. There was no effective system for keeping track of car keys—on a lot with hundreds of cars! The Profit Team developed a location system for keys and added $10,000 to the bottom line.

When do you see cars advertised in the paper? Usually on Saturdays and Sundays. But this car dealership was closed on Sundays, and there was no one there to answer telephone queries from prospective customers. The Profit Team arranged for sales people who are go-getters to have Sunday calls transferred to their homes on a rotating basis. Now the sales person answers the phone with the name of the dealership in the comfort of his or her home, and gains many new leads. Their ads now read, "Call for information on Sundays." As a result, sales people generated leads even on Sundays that generated an added $50,000 in bottom line potential.

The Profit Team discovered they were losing business because customers couldn't drop their cars off the night before for servicing. They hired night service "advisors" to handle night drop-offs quickly and courteously, so that customers no longer had to wait in long lines in the morning. This initiative, costing just several people's salaries, added thousands more in profit potential.

Service writers were wasting time searching for cars on the lot. The Profit Team had each parking space numbered and added $116,000 to the unrealized bottom line potential.

A new detailing service was added to the traditional car repair and servicing items for a new $100,000 in annual recurring profit. They also added a quick while-you-wait oil change and lubrication service. Not only did this program add the potential of $75,000 in revenue, but it allowed time for the dealership employees to "get to know" their customers while they waited, to establish a "donuts and coffee" relationship that helped build customer loyalty.

These are just a few initiatives this dealership's Profit Teams carried through from idea to completion. There is absolutely no doubt that effective implementation is absolutely vital to the Profit Enhancement Process to this dealership and to your business, too.

# Instant Replays

The more you get people to write down their commitments, the better chance you will have to win the Profit Game.

Project implementation is the key component of maximizing profit.

Clearly define each project and the steps needed to complete it.

Every Profit Champion needs support and the opportunity to consult with their PAL.

Each profit team is responsible for planning their own profit project.

No one, no matter how capable, will be able to implement profit strategies without the help of others in the organization.

Each team should build a consensus on how they want to work and what they plan to do, step by step, task by task.

Motivate your profit teams with a well-touted and fully understood reward program.

Bottom up—rather than top down—implementation is the key to winning the Profit Super Bowl.

Greater profitability comes when players know they are accountable, responsible, and will reap rewards for scoring profits or be penalized if they consistently fail to make it to the profit zone.

Profit Champions must be held accountable and know the limits of their authority.

Winning the Profit Super Bowl will bring hundreds of thousands—even millions—of dollars of previously unrealized profit to your bottom line.

# CHAPTER 6

# PROFIT IS THE SCORE

This whole experience has once again proven that you can never close the book on learning. The processes you have passed on to us for uncovering profit opportunities then setting time lines and completion dates to ensure achievement of the goals has been most rewarding to us. During my 25+ years in management, I would rank this experience among my most rewarding.

—Don Namuth, V.P./General Sales Manager, Forman Distributing Co.

---

Great profit coaches never rest on their laurels.

---

Whenever you think your company is as successful as it can be, remember those old slide rules from calculus class boldly imprinted with the name of the manufacturer—Pickett Slide Rule Company. Talk about having a market cornered. But Pickett's success apparently blinded them to the microprocessor, and calculators swiftly made Pickett's little sticks obsolete. They are collectibles in antique shops now. There are those who say that the seeds of a business's destruction are sown during good times. They may also say that the seeds to business success are sown during turbulent times, but great coaches never rest on their laurels. Instead they coach and seek input and feedback during good seasons and bad seasons, utilizing their Profit Teams.

Think about the National Cash Register Company. Their NCR logo dominated mechanical cash registers from coast to coast for decades. Now most of their handsome-but-bulky old cash registers are long gone, but NCR's emblem now decorates millions of computerized retail terminals. NCR changed with the times.

Netscape Communications Corp., the Internet software company that is Microsoft's fiercest competitor, had a rough 1997. What did their president, James L. Barksdale, do? He bucked the trend of ever-higher compensation for chief executives by forgoing his own salary and bonuses in 1997. He personally took the heat for the company's poor performance, and used this show of commitment to Netscape to spur his employees to work as hard as he does to beat Microsoft. He showed them and investors that he is willing to sacrifice because he believes in his company. That's commitment!

The answer is: Find new avenues for generating new business opportunities and increasing the bottom line. Changing with the times is vital and that means being open to new ideas, being flexible, and being in tune with the marketplace. Those ideas must come from the entire company, not just from management, but from every level of employees. Each company member must understand what the company is and does, and that he or she is part of the mission and vision now and in the future. In fact, their future depends on the company's products and services evolving with the times. It is possible that 50 percent of what you'll be selling five years from now may not even exist today—or that you don't know about it yet.

We once held a Profit Super Bowl for 15 executives of a management information business, including the CFO, executive secretary, marketing director, and branch and sales managers. When asked the question, "What does your company sell?" there were fifteen different answers.

After some discussion of the problem, we broke the group into five three-member teams. Each team was asked to come up with a new description of what the company sells. There were now five explanations instead of 15, still too many. Next, these managers voted on which of the five to eliminate as not meaningful enough. Two explanations survived the cuts, and the group merged these into a clear, concise statement.

Now when asked what the company sells, every one of the 150 employees in the firm can answer, "We sell management information solutions to business problems to assist our customers in being more competitive and profitable."

This was not an easy process. The owner of the business was so elated he went to call his mother. Laughing, he said, "For years she's asked what I do for a living. Until now I couldn't tell her!"

Every company also needs a clear understanding of its customers, products, markets, opportunities and challenges. In our years of experience as Profit Advisors, we have found that many of these can only be seen clearly by an "outsider," someone not intimately involved with "the ways things are done here" at that company. Such an advisor will also help to change the company's culture—its attitude toward progress and creative solutions. When engaged as the outside experts, we facilitate the identifying of opportunities that employees may be aware of but don't know how to articulate, bring these opportunities to light, act to create a forum for communication, and then assist the CEO in his or her profit coaching throughout the implementation process.

---

Your profit attitude determines your profit altitude.

---

We've seen it time and again. Once Profit Team members are made responsible for profits and develop a sense of their profit*ability*, then an overflowing river of ideas for unrealized profit potential starts to flow. We have defined profit*ability* as the skill to analyze your business and determine what more can be done to add value to the bottom line. PEP "dams" those ideas and puts them to work. With Profit Teams working to marshal the creative forces of the entire company, your company's chances to change and grow with the demands of the times are greatly enhanced.

This chapter is all about attitudes and answers. Why attitudes? Because we can't emphasize enough how positive attitudes plus positive actions equal positive results; and the opposite is also true. For PEP to work you've got to overcome the following:

---

"Departmentalism" destroys teamwork
and will destroy your chances for
winning the Profit Game.

---

We often engage the starting team at a Profit Super Bowl for automobile dealerships by asking the question: "If you could never run another big newspaper ad, how would you bring in customers?"

We ask this question because we've found that frequently auto dealerships have absolutely no impetus for one department to work with another department. There are so many clues that a customer may need a new car. In the service department, customers decide the estimate for repairing their old car is too high. In the warranty department, a customer's extended warranty runs out, leaving them financially exposed in case of a major service problem. In the leasing department, customer leases expire regularly. These are all opportunities to sell a satisfied customer a new car. But you can't capitalize on them unless all departments are communicating with each other and working with the sales department. Why didn't the service department inform the sales department that there was a customer with a new car need? Because, "It isn't my job and there's nothing in it for me." There is no profit process.

Usually during the Profit Super Bowl, newly profit*able* managers see that tremendous additional revenue will come simply from providing a way for the departments to work together. They understand that the culture of the company has defeated this objective. Often a Profit Team is appointed to develop a commission system for all departments so that sales referrals between departments are rewarded.

In one case, during the Profit Super Bowl, the group discussed how the dealership's telephone receptionist became very grumpy in late afternoon when all the service customers call in about their cars. This dealership now pays the receptionist $2 for every car sold as a result of her successfully routing a call to a salesman. This changed her entire attitude and made her part of the company's new profit culture. Her focus became customer service and sales, not just answering the telephone.

Departmentalism, or competition among departments, will defeat a company. Can you imagine a football team where the individual players decide their own moves and compete with each other for the ball? We tried to get the CEO of a systems integration firm we worked with to recognize that competition among her departments was killing the company. We found out when we performed the Profit Audit that multiple departments were so intent on trying to get sales that in some cases they were competing for the same customer with different prices. We alerted the CEO that she had major problems with department in-fighting and that there was no system for tracking who was working with which prospective customer. She just wouldn't recognize this as a problem. She was so intent on encouraging competition, she defeated herself. Unfortunately, the company went into bankruptcy.

---

"Always praise a player in front of his peers.
Never criticize him in public."
— Larry Pecattiello, Coach, Detroit Lions

---

Good people hold the answers your company needs to win the Profit Game. Managers need to encourage them, to work with them, so these opportunities will surface, not be buried under functional tasks and emergencies. What would your business be like if managers only got promoted when and if the people they supervised got promoted? You'd see a lot more managers managing the people who do the work, not just the work.

One of our most successful clients, a ready-mix, brick-and-block manufacturer and wholesale building materials company, has now held five Profit Super Bowls during the last seven years. The two years in which no Profit Super Bowl was held, their profits were static. In the five years they played in the Profit Super Bowl, profits were up. In the beginning, the CEO hired us because he knew there was much more profit potential in his company and was convinced his people had the answers, but he did not know how to tap that resource. At the end of the first Profit Super Bowl, when scores of ideas had been generated and a plan for new profit was in place, he looked us in the eye and sighed with relief. He had been right. More profit was there! It took the free forum provided by the Profit Super Bowl to flush those ideas out and renew everyone's responsibility in turning profit-generating ideas into financial results. Each year that we work with the company, we wind up with more-substantial issues than the year before because the Profit Team is now comprised of seasoned veterans who have learned to work and think profit*ably*. They are an all-star team of possibility thinkers.

---

Great coaches are never afraid
to admit they've made a mistake.

---

As an aside, this same CEO had launched the company into manufacturing concrete cemetery liners. After some years of losing money on the project, he had to admit he'd made a mistake. It was a money-losing venture. Where did he make this admission? He made it during one of the company's Profit Super Bowls. He admitted to us that this gathering of his star players gave him the courage to close the operation. That decision decreased his sales but increased his profits.

The Profit Enhancement Process is designed to provide a free forum for new profit ideas and a process for implementing them. One reason we wrote this book is because we've seen it proven so many times. When employees feel their ideas are welcome, that there is a viable way to submit them and rewards for doing so, they become profit*able*. The opposite is also true.

Unfortunately, we can't say every Profit Super Bowl has been an absolute success. An engineering firm whose business was heavily dependent on government contracts called us in because the CEO knew there was profit*ability* the company wasn't tapping. During the Profit Audit it became clear that 50 percent of the company's problems could be attributed to the vice president who was a 50 percent owner in the firm. Everyone disliked him because he was a "control freak" who bullied people. During the Profit Super Bowl he dominated every discussion and wouldn't let anyone else talk. Despite all of our efforts, he refused to let the meeting be a free forum, without fear of retribution.

Even so, discussion revealed that one of the main revenue problems for the firm was in allocating costs for government contracts. Many of those who did the work did not understand the difference between direct cost and indirect cost allocation. The Profit Team identified $500,000 in potential profits. But Harry the Bullying VP interfered again. He shouted out, "I can't believe you don't know this. It's so basic!" So, what happened? The group clammed up. Afterwards, Harry wouldn't give the Profit Team the time to discover the firm's billing opportunities. And, when we urged the CEO to step in and let his team proceed, he wouldn't do it. He chose Harry, the other shareholder, over his employees, and this firm is losing the Profit Game.

---

PEP focuses everyone on the profits needed to grow the company and add value to it.

---

You may have founded the company and built it to what it is today. You know your business inside and out. How can someone else identify something you don't already know about your own business—whether it's a Profit Advisor like us or your very own employees? Maybe there is some hidden profit you can't find in there, but your company is doing all right, maybe even successful or super-successful.

Trust us. We've seen the Profit Enhancement Process work so many times. Most of our clients are entrepreneurial companies that have a burning desire to do it better and know it can be improved! More than half of the companies we've coached in the past have come back for additional Profit Super Bowls. PEP doesn't interfere at all with their own strategic goals for the company. It enhances them, makes them work faster, focuses everyone on the profits they need to build the company and add value to it. Our number-one successes have been with profit*able* companies with competitive coaches who know there are even more opportunities to improve the score.

Unfortunately, the opposite is also true. We were hired to facilitate a Profit Super Bowl for a news service company. Strangely enough, the COO asked that the CEO not be there, and during the meeting that COO was not very complimentary about his boss or about any part of the Profit Enhancement Process. We considered this situation so dangerous that we asked to meet privately with the CEO to inform him about this. We were convinced that the COO was truly not a leader and was, in fact, undermining the progress of the company. We warned the owner that the COO was working behind his back. He didn't want the grief of dealing with his COO, so he didn't take the time to deal with the problem. The Profit Plan developed during the Profit Super Bowl was never implemented. Unhappily, the company's sales have dropped by more than two-thirds, and it may not be around to play next season.

---

PEP provides the support and monitoring of progress that effective implementation requires.

---

In the previous chapter we've gone through the implementation process and emphasized its importance. PEP provides the support and monitoring of progress that implementation requires. It is vital that the Profit Activities Leader meet regularly with Profit Champions to measure progress and to help them successfully complete their profit projects. The Profit Activities Leader should, of course, be a person who has the vision to see the whole picture. He or she must have profit*ability*, the ability to recognize business opportunities and the talent to turn ideas into results. They must be commited to the Profit Enhancement Process and have the project-managing and people-managing skills necessary to coach the best out of their players.

The PAL needs support, too—from the CEO and from his own profit coach. Part of our profit advising coaching role is to be "industrial psycho-profit therapists." We listen, we work with you, and we provide a fresh perspective on the profit projects because we aren't caught up with the everyday operations of the business. We do not have a vested interest in the past.

Recently we saw a big ad for a going-out-of-business sale held by a furniture store. We knew the owner. Unhappily, he had not understood the benefits of the Profit Enhancement Process when he had explained it to him some years ago. The CEO said he didn't need our services because he knew he was doing everything that could be done for the company. He didn't have profit*ability*. His team of employees probably had profit*able* solutions, but no way to present them. They were never asked. Now the business is closed.

---

Players play harder when they know their work will be rewarded.

---

When people know what's in it for them, do you think they're eager to put in the extra effort working on new profit initiatives? You bet. And it doesn't always have to be big monetary rewards, although money is still a strong motivator. Sometimes it takes making them feel like a real part of the profit process—to make everyone an official Profit Enhancement Officer.

We worked with a family-owned catering company that had some real problems, both financial and personal family ones. They were so busy squabbling among themselves that they couldn't even agree on a common strategy for the company. Our first major task was to help the family determine which role each was to play in the company's management, then to get them motivated to win the Profit Game. Once they felt comfortable with each other, this commitment was easy to obtain.

Our client later reported that we engaged them "...in some difficult, thought-provoking and probing questions...very needed questions regarding commitment, performance, expectations and individual and collective goals for our business." He went on to say:

> My brother and I, after some coaching, and an overall meeting of minds, have taken on the leadership role of the company along with our operations manager,

> now general manager, who is entering his 26th year of service with us. Our highly experienced events management staff, each with over 15 years of service, has also taken on a leadership role and now has many more avenues and opportunities for input and growth.

Then we assembled their all-star employees for the Profit Super Bowl. Many of these loyal people had never before been asked to participate in any kind of profit strategizing session for the future of the company. It was exciting to see them begin to light up with ideas and to offer them freely when given the chance.

At the end of the session, the family issues were resolved, their employees were involved in and committed to the bottom line growth of the company, and everyone's new ideas were incorporated into a true Profit Plan for action. This company went from a loss to a pre-tax profit of $200,000. Now the company has scheduled a Profit Super Bowl for each annual planning process. They use their slow time of the year to devote themselves to identifying and implementing profit-making projects. This client wrote afterwards:

> The tough issues that were affecting the company have been identified and are being dealt with. There is a renewal level and excitement and optimism now in the company. We are well on our way to realizing the profit potential of our long-held and successful family business, so that it will thrive well into future generations.

WOW!

---

Often it's the shoemaker's kids who are the ones going without shoes.

---

It's amazing how many service companies claim to be working to improve the profit*ability* of their clients while forgetting about their own. We were looking over the sales materials of a hospitality software firm we worked with. Their promotional brochure touted their goal as developing new products to make their customers more profitable. They even boasted, "Our employees are focused on profit."

This company has offices all around the world. When we gave our Profit Enhancement Survey to 65 of them, gathered for a meeting, their scores were in the ones and twos across the board, out of a possible 10, on the statement, "Our employees are focused on generating bottom line opportunities and have a plan to follow." What an eye-opener this aspect of the Profit Audit was to the owners!

This company provides worldwide services and advertises that they are interested in improving profit for their clients, but their employees realize that the company has no profit plan for itself or for them.

---

PEP supports your company's strategic goals. It doesn't change them; it enhances them with the bottom line results of additional opportunities.

---

The big difference between the Profit Enhancement Process and other management systems is that we're not suggesting you change your firm's strategic goals, just to define, refine, and hone them for your employees and your customers. You know who you want to be, and important members of your team need to be reading from the same playbook. PEP makes sure you achieve the results you are capable of for the benefit of the owners, employees, families, lenders, suppliers, and customers of your business.

PEP can make a difference NOW. It helps you identify unrealized profits that in many cases have immediate bottom line results, while others may take some time to achieve. We're not promising that you'll always pull in thousands of extra profit dollars immediately, although sometimes a brilliant profit strategy can do just that. Like the trash company story where all it took to realize $78,000 extra was to get the trash men to get off the truck when it was weighed at the landfill. Others do take longer. Like the automobile dealership where $225,000 was generated over a year's time when a new repair-parts ordering system was put in place so mechanics didn't waste time waiting in line at the parts counter. They're not always complex initiatives. Sometimes they are simple ones, like the restaurant chain that measured the size of its trash receptacle, found that the actual cubic yards were less than it was being charged by the hauler, and saved $60,000 by stopping this practice. The Profit Enhancement Process brings all these ideas together—the big ideas and the little ones—to provide your company with identifiable steps to obtain hidden profit opportunities. Remember TIMES x TIMES x TIMES equals Endless Profit Opportunities. Your profit journey must be on the road to continued success. If you don't know where you are going, it doesn't matter which road you take. We want you to win every season. Profit is a business's lifetime journey, not a quick destination.

As opposed to other systems, you could say ours is a "grounds up" rather than a "trickle down" approach to bringing in extra profit, because PEP makes profit everyone's responsibility. We believe that everyone can be coached and trained to be profit*able.*

---

Great coaches learn from other winning teams.

---

Here are just a few of the great ideas and opportunities for extra profit that have already come out of the Profit Enhancement Process—opportunities that might be just what you and your business have been looking for.

### The Profit Advisors' Client Success Stories

1. **Automobile dealership** shutdown unnecessary utilities during closed hours. Estimated profit potential: $50,000.

2. **Office equipment dealer** created a process to eliminate billing omissions that were resulting from hand-written tickets not being entered into the computer. Estimated profit potential: $180,000.

3. **Printer** developed a process to verify that work orders are complete and accurate prior to being placed into production. Estimated profit potential: $40,000.

4. **Professional service firm** developed a procedure to catch work that was not originally authorized. This eliminated a problem with uncollectible bills. Estimated profit potential: $125,000.

5. **Employment agency** combined multiple invoices into one envelope rather than separately mailing them. Estimated profit potential: $4,000.

6. **Automotive service agency** initiated a regular customer satisfaction survey and was able to more effectively gauge customers' actual feelings. There was a noticeable improvement in additional business from existing customers. Estimated profit potential: $100,000.

7. **National advocacy group** reduced the paper size used for their magazine by one-eighth of an inch to a standard paper size. Estimated profit potential: $18,000.

8. **Food distributor** redefined the roles of their sales staff and added merchandising specialists. Estimated profit potential: $325,000.

9. **Accounting firm** developed a training program to educate employees in all of the products and services they offer. This cross-selling effort increased sales in all departments. Estimated profit potential: $75,000.

10. **Plumbing supply distributor** reduced permanent overtime through more effective scheduling and by requiring that employees get approval for extra hours before they are incurred. Estimated profit potential: $110,000.

11. **Retail tire company** established a "Red Carpet Service" to provide pick-up and delivery service for business people who

could not get away from their office to purchase tires. Estimated profit potential: $100,000.

12. **Liquor distributor** segmented a third of one component of their product line that could justify higher prices than their normal markup percentage. Estimated profit potential: $350,000.

13. **Law firm** established a protocol to enhance the efficiency of staff meetings. The resulting guidelines better utilized the time of attending staff and eliminated necessary and/or unproductive meetings. Estimated profit potential: $ 40,000.

14. **Computer training company** restructured their processes for selling to customers. Estimated profit potential: $500,000.

15. **Medical laboratory** identified a new system to archive medical records and modified the policies relating to record retention and file maintenance. Estimated profit potential: $250,000.

16. **Beverage distributor** increased the on-street time of their sales force by establishing clear guidelines and limiting their role in personally handling last-minute deliveries. This resulted in additional sales without hiring additional sales people. Estimated profit potential: $250,000.

17. **Trade association** negotiated a credit card affinity program for their members. Estimated profit potential: $1,000,000.

18. **Clothing retailer** took quality employees from one branch, on a temporary basis, to help train individuals at another. Estimated profit potential: $170,000.

19. **Office supply distributor** identified additional items that could be sold with each telephone order and incorporated a training program for their customer service representatives to ensure successful implementation. Estimated profit potential: $200,000.

**20. Computer graphics firm** contacted their suppliers to help organize and fund a training program to improve their dealers' operations. Estimated profit potential: $95,000.

**21. Card and gift store** created sales analysis and profit*ability* reports by product line to more quickly notice pertinent trends. Estimated profit potential: $15,000.

**22. Concrete block manufacturer** developed a plan to eliminate paying for the weight of water in raw materials delivered in trucks during wet weather. Estimated profit potential: $50,000.

**23. Landscaping contractor** developed a plan to obtain more off-season work. Estimated profit potential: $72,000.

**24. Cleaning service** established English classes for their ethnically diverse workforce. Breakdowns in communication impacted quality control, timely deliveries and ultimately customer satisfaction. Estimated profit potential: $100,000.

**25. Auto body repair shop** extended hours for estimates to evenings and weekends to make the process more convenient for working customers. Estimated profit potential: $50,000.

**26. Trash hauler** got their drivers to get out of the trash truck while the truck and its load of trash were getting weighed at the landfill. Estimated profit potential: $78,000.

**27. Lighting supply company** had owners of vendor companies come to their office to pick up their accounts payable check. When on the premises, they got a tour of the facilities. Expanded business and some new customers were the results. Estimated profit potential: $27,000.

**28. Medical supply company** revamped their phone system to be more user-friendly for customers and allow easier access to customer service representatives. A couple of lost sales per week are now saved. Estimated profit potential: $500,000.

**29. Advertising agency** started using an e-mail system instead of paper memos to its staff. Estimated profit potential: $25,000.

**30. Moving and storage company** set up a procedure to call three days prior to appointments to confirm. This resulted in more qualified meetings and a higher close rate. Estimated profit potential: $40,000.

**31. Wholesale bakery** revised their shift management system to minimize inefficient interdepartmental interactions. Emphasis included: job descriptions, scheduling, accountability, measurement and training. Estimated profit potential: $700,00.

**32. Specialty food manufacturer** consolidated similar recipes to reduce the number of short production runs. This reduced line cleaning and raised the size of production runs. Estimated profit potential: $500,000.

**33. Tool fabricator** organized a maintenance and storage plan for equipment that moved between departments. Estimated profit potential: $54,000.

**34. Health and beauty aids supply company** increased their prices by ten cents a case. Their customers did not notice the increase because the per item cost was less than a penny. Estimated profit potential: $130,000.

**35. Public relations firm** started tracking when work came in versus work being delivered, so they could react more quickly to poor sales trends. Estimated profit potential: $130,000.

**36. Automation control manufacturer** focused on obtaining job tax credits for hiring certain types of workers. Estimated profit potential: $24,000.

**37. Advertising agency** developed a new system for tracking business prospects to facilitate adequate and timely follow-up. Estimated profit potential: $120,000.

**38. Technical services company** coordinated travel through one travel agency and established corporate guidelines. Estimated profit potential: $120,000.

**39. Embroidery company** created an incentive program for unused sick days. Estimated profit potential: $7,500.

**40. Medical laboratory** set ordering guidelines and standards for supplies. Estimated profit potential: $500,000.

**41. Language school** created an internal referral fee for recruiting new candidates and reduced employment agency charges. Estimated profit potential: $32,000.

**42. Book distributor** designed a new employee orientation and training program in order to increase retention levels. Estimated profit potential: $140,000.

**43. Home accessory store** converted an unused second floor into retail space and rented it to another business. Estimated profit potential: $125,000.

**44. Sign maintenance company** paid a referral fee to employees who informed them of the names of companies with burned-out business signs. Estimated profit potential: $15,000.

**45. Temporary employment agency** coordinated classified advertising with their branch offices and centrally purchased these services and consolidated ads. Estimated profit potential: $608,000.

**46. Home remodeler** created premium pricing for handyman jobs by scheduling jobs during evenings and weekends. Estimated profit potential: $37,000.

**47. Courier service** reduced vendor costs for phones, beepers and radios by consolidating contracts and establishing rules for usage. Estimated profit potential: $100,000.

**48. Janitorial supply company** developed a driver checklist as a means of spotting additional sales opportunities. Estimated profit potential: $75,000.

**49. Hospital out-patient clinic** overbooked appointments based on no-show statistics and increased the number of patients served with no staff increase. Estimated profit potential: $320,000.

**50. Payroll service** generated extra fees by offering customized management reports for customers. Estimated profit potential: $40,000.

**51. Metal fabricating company** created an "adopt-an-area" program for employees accepting responsibility for keeping their workplace clean and performing minor equipment maintenance. Estimated profit potential: $55,000.

**52. Roofing contractor** installed a process to retrieve unused materials from job sites. Estimated profit potential: $180,000.

How do we bring out ideas during the Profit Enhancement Process—through leadership and questions, right? Bright, creative people with positive attitudes often need just the right questions to get them digging into their own experiences and working to find the answers. One of our clients, a specialty gas supply company, hired us to help them reach their goal of growing their bottom line by 20 percent. In a wide-ranging discussion of sales opportunities, someone noted that if the company had more gas cylinders, they could sell more. The problem was having to spend $340,000 a year to replenish liquid gas cylinders. Without that expense, they could make their sales goal. Customers simply weren't returning the cylinders that were nominally rented to them. Replacements cost $160 each.

A Profit Champion was appointed to dig into this problem. The team he put together discovered that the delivery drivers were more focused on timely delivery of cylinders than worrying about making pickups of the empties at the same time. If the empties weren't conveniently there to return, they didn't worry about it. It was just a custom in their industry. The team reasoned that while drivers couldn't really help them raise sales with their customers, they could become more diligent in picking up empty cylinders and save the company $160 for each one returned. So they suggested that drivers be awarded 60 cents for each returned cylinder up to the quantity originally delivered and $1.20 for each cylinder returned in excess of those they delivered. Amazingly, the company soon had too many cylinders for their warehouse. Savings in replacement cylinders added $340,000 of profit to the company's bottom line during the first year.

PEP does not change the strategic goals of the company. It changes the culture in which people work. It encourages everyone to become aware of profit opportunities and to find ways of implementing them. It develops their profit*ability* so they will add value to the company without reinventing its mission.

---

Employees are your most valuable resource.
Coach them into a winning Profit Team.

---

A big "Eureka!" we've found from facilitating Profit Super Bowls is that in many companies no one is responsible at the end of the day for their employees' successes or failures. Many entrepreneurial companies don't even have a system for personnel evaluation. People don't know which direction to travel. They are trying to score touchdowns, but don't know toward which end zone to run.

During the Profit Super Bowl for a distribution firm, we facilitated a discussion about their problem with low employee retention. The firm employed 170 employees: two-thirds of them were telephone customer service reps, one-third filled orders, but in all only 20 percent had worked for the company longer than one year. Because of this rapid turnover, managers spent their time putting out fires, filling the gaps left by absent or resigned employees. Further discussion revealed that the phone staff had no benefits—no training, no health insurance, no job descriptions, no orientation classes. The "Improve

Employee Retention" initiative that came out of the Profit Super Bowl, was to appoint Profit Teams with Champions to address these issues. One team was established to develop orientation classes designed to help new employees understand the work of the company, the products they sold, and their place in it before they began talking to customers on the phone. Another team was charged with establishing a three-month evaluation program for new employees. Health insurance benefits were awarded to those who made the cuts and became permanent members of the team. A third team worked on a program of monthly training sessions to keep employees informed about new products and customer service techniques and to support their sense of pride in their work. The profit potential of this initiative was $190,000.

Even when they are leaving your employ, employees can tell you a lot about the state of your company. We advise our clients to hold exit interviews with employees leaving the company. Remember, perceptions are real. The way former employees view your organization may be the way things really are. Take these comments seriously! Here is a sample questionnaire we've developed for our clients.

## FUTURE PROFIT OPPORTUNITIES
### Employee Exit Questionnaire

Name of Company______________________________
Department______________________________
Employee______________________________Date____________

1. Why are you leaving the firm? (Check those items that apply.)

| | | | |
|---|---|---|---|
| ❑ | Pay | ❑ | More responsibility |
| ❑ | Job Promotion | ❑ | Type of work |
| ❑ | More convenient hours | ❑ | Supervision |
| ❑ | Coworkers | ❑ | Office environment |
| ❑ | My physical condition | ❑ | Commuting distance |
| ❑ | Less responsibility | ❑ | Other (Specify) |
| | | | ______________________ |

2. If you are going to work for another firm, what are they offering you that we haven't?

3. Please rate the following:

Quality of product or services offered for sale.

*Outstanding* ❑ *Above Average* ❑ *Average* ❑ *Below Average* ❑

Competence of staff and management

*Outstanding* ❑ *Above Average* ❑ *Average* ❑ *Below Average* ❑

Opportunities for advancement

*Outstanding* ❑ *Above Average* ❑ *Average* ❑ *Below Average* ❑

Training

*Outstanding* ❑ *Above Average* ❑ *Average* ❑ *Below Average* ❑

Compensation and fringe benefits

*Outstanding* ❑ *Above Average* ❑ *Average* ❑ *Below Average* ❑

4. Was your workload a problem? (Too much or too little?)

5. Did you have the support (coaching, equipment, and technology) to be as effective as you are capable of?

6. What did you like most about your job?

7. What did you find most frustrating about your position?

8. In what areas could you have benefited from additional training?

9. Will you recommend our firm to prospective employees?

10. Will you recommend our firm to prospective customers?

Please share any other comments you have to help us be a model employer in the future.

Note: *Thanks for your valued services while employed by our organization.*

Organizational Structure—
Is your staff organized to work effectively?

A moving and storage company was determined to grow their sales. They hired us to coach them through the Profit Enhancement Process. We discovered during the Profit Audit phase of our engagement that their sales representatives were spending only about 12 1/2 percent of their time actually selling. The rest of the time was spent doing administrative and other non-sales related work. The company planned to hire more sales reps. They thought more sales people would mean more sales. Their current sales staff was frustrated. When the managers gathered for the Profit Super Bowl, this was an issue they chose to address, and they appointed a Profit Champion to review all the administrative and non-sales related work their sales reps were performing and suggest which tasks could be eliminated and reassigned to the administrative staff. The sales personnel now spend 80 percent of their time selling. Estimated profit potential? $250,000 annually.

There is nothing more unprofitable than making unnecessary work more efficient.

The Profit Audit we performed for a bank (jointly with another Institute of Profit Advisors member) revealed that they had too many employees by industry standards, but the employees' surveys revealed that they were feeling overworked. When we began to discuss this issue at the Profit Super Bowl, people were fearful that if the bank began letting the weaker people go and kept just the good people, they too would be overwhelmed and leave. So together we started focusing on what work could be eliminated, and it soon became clear that there was too much duplication and unnecessary work. There is nothing more unprofitable than making unnecessary work more efficient.

For instance, when the computer system had been installed ten years before, someone told the staff to keep duplicate records until they had confidence in the new system. They were still keeping duplicate records because no one had told them to stop!

Fortuitously, the internal auditor for the bank was one of the attendees at this Profit Super Bowl. As the discussion continued about what other work could be eliminated, people kept saying, "But the auditor requires this." More frequently than not, the auditor would speak up and say, "No, I don't!" Immediately, long-held beliefs about workload were eliminated along with work.

Every branch had their own office-supply vendors. A Profit Team was appointed to develop a central buying system to eliminate duplicate work in the branches and take advantage of bulk-purchase opportunities.

There were many, many unnecessary meetings. Few employees used their e-mail or telephones to communicate effectively, so they had meetings. A Profit Team was appointed to set up a training program for the e-mail and voice-mail systems.

There were too many duplicate reporting systems. The bank mailed out receipts for deposits made through the ATM system. Since customers can see their deposit records right on their monthly statement, this duplication was eliminated. There was a lack of efficiency in the way loan documents were prepared and too much unnecessary information was kept in the loan files. A Profit Team was established to develop a better system.

Thousands of customer telephone calls came in every month after Social Security checks were issued. Every month it was the same query: "Did my Social Security check get credited to my account?" Now the bank has an automated telephone system which answers Social Security direct-deposit questions automatically along with other common questions.

What did the elimination of duplicate work mean to this bank's bottom line? Sixty-six percent potential for improvement to their bottom line, year in and year out. They are diligently turning their unrealized bottom line potential into a financial reality.

Marketing & Sales —Are your sales people getting enough chances to run with the ball?

When we analyze the sales and marketing section during a Profit Audit, we always ask ourselves and the CEO: "Are your sales people getting enough chances to run with the ball?" We ask this because we firmly believe in the old saying, "Sales is a number's game." The more people you face, the better the chances are that you will make sales if coached properly. This is half correct. Success in sales is dependent on two things: activities and execution. If the receivers are thrown the football but aren't skilled and coached properly, it is unlikely they will execute the big plays that make all the difference in winning the Profit Game.

If you can't measure it, you can't track it and you can't manage it.

During the Profit Audit we conducted for a computer software training company, it soon became clear that there were severe weaknesses in the sales and marketing end of the business. The managers didn't know how to change the way the department was doing business in order to achieve their sales objectives. We learned from the managers that sales were posted at the end of the month, but sales people had no idea how they were performing during the rest of the month. The sales team was like a football team playing hard, not knowing what the score was until the game ended. They never knew whether they were winning or losing until it was too late to make a difference.

We coached the Profit Team on setting up a system for posting daily sales figures. Everyone on the sales staff now sees at a glance how their sales compare with delivery targets set for specific points of time during the current and future months. The numbers immediately illustrate how individuals and the group are performing. There are no surprises anymore. Everyone tracks their progress and makes adjustments to their game plan before it is too late to reach their profit goals.

A distribution company incorporated the same concept and added an additional twist—a tracking system for lost accounts that pinpoints drops in customer activity. The system alerts managers of customer accounts when there is a reduction in frequency of transactions. Now the company can more quickly discover problem accounts. They immediately determine what is causing the customer to change their buying patterns. The company now retains a significantly higher percentage of potentially lost business. This project has the profit potential of $250,000 extra for the bottom line this year, next year, and every subsequent year.

---

Sales feed egos, but profits feed families.

---

We advise Profit Teams to look at the bottom line of the income statement. A company is very fortunate to have a 10-percent bottom line net income. In other words, to earn $100,000 of additional profit, a company may have to increase sales by $1 million. So, the questions is: What if you were to cut costs by 10 percent instead? Let's check out the following hypothetical (and admittedly simplistic) example:

| | Pro Forma Prior to Cost Cutting or Increasing Sales | Pro Forma After Cutting Costs 10% | Pro Forma for Increasing Sales (Equivalent to Cutting Costs 10%) |
|---|---|---|---|
| **Sales** | $20,000,000 | $20,000,000 | $38,000,000 |
| **Cost of sales** | (10,000,000) | ( 9,000,000) | (19,000,000) |
| **Gross Profit** | **10,000,000** | **11,000,000** | **19,000,000** |
| **Operating Expenses** | (8,000,000) | (7,200,000) | (15,200,000) |
| **NET PROFIT** | **2,000,000** | **3,800,000** | **3,800,000** |

As you can see, cutting costs by 10 percent almost doubled the net profit. On the other hand, to increase profits to $3,800,000 without the 10-percent cost cutting, sales would have to increase to $38 million. Imagine the effort and cost associated with a sales increase of $18 million!

Many companies cannot afford to do business at nearly twice their existing volume, simply because they don't have enough cash to finance the sales increase. A sale made at the beginning of the month, for example, might not produce cash for 60 days, perhaps longer. In fact, sales might have to be greater than $38 million in this example, because the costs to finance the increased sales activity may be substantial.

While savings can be associated with greater volume. Realistically, all costs do not go up in proportion to the increased sales. Significant sales growth, however, might strain equipment and personnel, so profits might be minimized.

Consider sales increases along with adequate expense controls. This balance will provide the greatest bottom line benefit to your business.

---

Cross-Sell—Sell all of your products all of the time. What are you providing free that you can charge for?

---

A company selling supplies and equipment to the physically challenged asked us to help them increase their sales. A department manager in attendance at the Profit Super Bowl reported the following incident. She was servicing a long-time wheelchair repair customer and noticed that it was a new chair, but not one sold by her company. She asked her customer why he hadn't bought it from them. Surprised, he said that he didn't know that wheelchairs were included in her company's product line. It seems that he had only been in the repair department. This organization's selling price per wheelchair ranges from several hundred to several thousand dollars. Imagine how many dollars of lost sales may occur in your organization because customers don't know what you sell.

The Profit Team promptly appointed a Profit Champion and committee to address this problem, soon to become an opportunity. They devised a two-step plan. First, a product folder was assembled, containing informational material on the variety of products and services offered by the company. Now whenever a customer enters the showroom, he or she is given this full-product brochure. Then the customer is offered a tour of the company's impressive facility. The Profit Team developed the major jobs and services highlights for this tour; and customer service representatives were trained in performing the walk-through so that when a customer mentions a need, they steer her to the right department. The Profit Team uncovered these missed sales opportunities, and the profit project team established simple procedures to maximize sales and services which are provided to their customers. The company wins, the customer wins, the vendor wins, the employees win!

An additional "discovery" generated substantial additional revenue for this company, with little cost. They published a free monthly newsletter on news and products of interest to the physically challenged. One employee who is physically challenged himself asked why this publication was free to subscribers when it provided such valuable information. No one had an answer. Three months later, the company began selling subscriptions. This "grounds up" initiative brought $200,000 in previously unrealized profit potential (with little additional effort or expense) which had previously been invisible to top management. They made the invisible visible.

---

Pricing—The customer is the driving force when it comes to selling prices.

---

Customers will pay you what they think your product or service is worth, not a penny more. Traditionally, many businesses have priced their goods and services based on cost. Cost is irrelevant in the buying decision of the purchaser. They never know the cost. Understanding this basic yet all-important principle is essential to determining the real profit opportunities in your business. Your organization's gross margin potential is illustrated using the following model:

| | | |
|---|---|---|
| **Potential Sales** | = | **Units sold X customer's perceived value per unit** |
| **<Cost of Sales>** | = | **Accurately determined direct and indirect costs of product/services sold** |
| **Gross Margin Potential** | | **The dollars left to pay all other expenses as well as generate profits** |

Unless your customers perceive that your product is truly unique, you've got to remain competitive in pricing goods and services. Even uniqueness, however, has limits in what customers are willing to pay. Make sure you know your competitors, what they sell, and what they charge.

Pricing decisions must work in concert with other strategic business decisions. Think about your sales goals, corporate image, marketing strategies, competitor goals, and various other related business objectives. Put those business objectives in writing and share that information with your Profit Team. Profit Team members will then be able to make informed critical pricing decisions.

Here's a last quick sales idea. In an effort to create new sales leads for their company, one of our distribution clients created a training program to help its truck drivers spot sales opportunities while making deliveries. Now the drivers track their discoveries on a form that is kept with them in their trucks. When they return to the warehouse, they give the form to their supervisor, who then forwards it to the sales staff. The drivers receive a commission on any new sales that result from their efforts, and the estimated profit potential: $100,000.

---

Create a whole new profit culture
where your Profit Team keeps scoring.

---

We've said this over and over again, the Profit Enhancement Process is a journey. It is meant to create a new profit culture, a whole new way of thinking and working that doesn't interfere with the long-term goals of the company, but produces a never-ending stream of new ideas from your people who have profit*ability*. Most often these ideas don't involve major restructuring, just profit*ability*.

For instance, the use of corporate procurement cards for purchasing is increasing because they minimize paperwork, thus eliminating unnecessary overhead. Since purchasing functions by necessity are transaction-oriented, eliminating any of these time-consuming activities while controlling costs would offer a company significant extra profits. Well-run companies have traditionally used a purchase order system to establish purchasing controls. By spending less time with unnecessary paperwork, purchasing agents can spend more time on buying strategies. Smart companies we work with have established purchasing policies that permit the use of corporate procurement credit cards for amounts below predetermined limits.

Remember the Paredo 20/80 rule? Twenty percent of the variables produce 80 percent of the results. In most cases, 20 percent of what you buy represents 80 percent of what the company spends. It represents only 20 percent of the cost associated with processing the paperwork. Using the procurement credit card for 80 percent of your purchases, which represent 20 percent of your expenditures, will save 80 percent of the company's cost of processing paperwork. Of course, the purchasing department must develop procedures for using the card, develop financial reports to assure compliance and reporting are adequate, and establish adequate internal control procedure before this program is put in place.

Our clients report that the average purchase costs from $30 to $300 in administrative expenses. Using this procedure, these costs can be reduced 80 to 90 percent, and the savings goes directly to your bottom line.

Some creative companies earn air miles by using procurement credit cards. The earned air miles reduce their travel costs. Combining travel cost savings with administrative cost savings will make the procurement credit card an excellent alternative to your other more costly methods of administratively handling the procurement functions.

---

Some winning plays for your playbook.

---

A manufacturing company changed many aspects of its operating procedures and realized millions of dollars in extra profit potential. All of these ideas came out of their first Profit Super Bowl where their starting Profit Team developed true profit*ability*.

This manufacturer sells to the giant hardware store chains. The Profit Team determined that one of their greatest profit fumbles was delivering partial loads on their trucks. They set up some real financial incentives to encourage their customers to buy full loads or share the delivery with other stores. This initiative added an extra $116,000 in previously unrealized bottom line potential by saving delivery expenses.

The Profit Team identified a weakness in their customer service department: The receptionist and other telephone-answering staff were not really trained to answer questions about the company's products, nor did they know who else might answer each question. "That's not my job," they would say as they handed the call on to the next uniformed employee. The Profit Team determined which were the most frequently-asked customer questions, and set up a program to train operators about the products and issues and who could answer each question. In addition, the company had no sales tracking database. The Profit Team established one and generated an extra $425,000 in profit potential the first year.

Consider testing your own system by calling your business phone number as a customer in disguise. You might be astonished about the sales opportunities your firm is losing because of untrained and ineffective procedures for handling customer requests and inquiries that can potentially turn into additional sales. Your phone system mannerisms and technology may need improving as well in order to ensure a predictable result.

Our client had not trained customer service representatives to cross-sell their products. The company sold certain products to some customers, and different products to others. The Profit Team developed a new sales program in which all the company's products were featured in customer promotional materials. Cross-selling has brought in an extra $300,000 in potential profit.

The company purchased its raw materials by weight. The Profit Team discovered that they were buying truckloads of raw materials with high moisture content. They set moisture content limits for raw materials. This reduced costs and saved the company $100,000.

In addition, they now have a Profit Champion in charge of repairing the wooden palettes on which their products are shipped and stored. Instead of throwing away broken palettes, this profit*able* employee repairs and recycles them. No one was in charge of managing the surface utilization of the palettes. Some were only 70-percent utilized. The Profit Team evaluated the size of palettes and compared them against the size and weight of their products. This maximized storage and minimized delivery expenses. The extra profit potential generated from these two initiatives is $80,000.

A Profit Team examined the pricing on their inventories. They looked at the pricing for their products based on availability and quality. Accordingly, they raised some prices and lowered others, and developed close-out procedures for excess inventory. These initiatives brought in $180,000 in extra cash.

The company had no procedure for validating the accuracy of orders. This created many costly errors. The Profit Team put new control procedures in place and greatly reduced those error rates.

There was no preventative maintenance plan for the company's equipment. We know that preventative maintenace prolongs the life of equipment and keeps people working instead of waiting for equipment to be repaired. The Profit Team established a plan for preventative equipment maintenance and saved the company a potential of $260,000 in excess repair costs, wasted time, and the inability to fill orders promptly.

Now add it all up. This company through its Profit Teams "found" $1,161,000 of unrealized profit for their bottom line.

Just think what you can do for your company.

---

14 Things You Can Do Today to Drive Profits to Your Bottom Line.

---

1. If your business is seasonal, ask your biggest vendors to let you stock up now, but pay when your customers buy. Also, renegotiate your leases to pay only those 8, 9, or 10 months out of the year when you experience the greatest sales. See how well your cash flow improves.

2. During the next two weeks, keep a list of products your customers would have bought had you stocked them. Then calculate how much revenue you will earn by stocking the three most-requested items.

3. Ask your employees to make a list of ten ways they would like to be rewarded for a job well done. See how much you will make by awarding these perks, instead of giving subjective cash bonuses.

4. Ask your production foreman to estimate how much you spend in lost production, manufacturing errors leading to rework, and injuries. Then calculate how much extra profit will come by offering manufacturing crews a percentage of the savings from waste and accidents they prevent.

5. Tell your plant foreman to give you a list of equipment that is idle most of the time. Then calculate how much you will save in insurance, property taxes, maintenance, storage space and carrying charges by getting rid of it.

6. Ask your secretaries, delivery people, janitor, customer service personnel, shipping clerks, production workers, service people, paralegals, staff accountants—anyone who performs the day-to-day work in your business—to write down five ways your company can become more profit*able*. See how many bottom line ideas you receive.

7. Start sending letters to customers who discontinue doing business with you thanking them for their past patronage. See how many call you to reinstate their account.

8. Ask your accounting department to rank your customers by dollars they spend. Calculate how much more money you will make by transferring your time and dollars from servicing the lowest-producing 80 percent to "wowing" the top 20 percent of your customers beyond their wildest expectations.

9. Ask your accounting department to tell you how much you spent last year on overnight priority packages and shipping. Then calculate how much you will save if 75 percent of those are sent to arrive the following afternoon instead of morning.

10. Ask your payroll manager to give you a list of employees who were paid overtime last year. Initiate a bonus to selected employees in those departments who get their work done responsibly without incurring any overtime. See how much that will add to your bottom line.

11. If you currently bill customers a fixed amount every month, calculate how much you'll save in monthly mailing costs and how much you'll increase cash flow by billing in advance every two months instead.

12. Calculate how much you spent last year for products and services that could have been billed, but were not authorized by your customers. See how much you will make with a system to catch what is not authorized before it occurs and get your customer's approval in advance.

13. Calculate how much more you will earn if you improve your net pre-tax by just 10 percent.

14. Make a list of all the things you will do with those extra profits!

# Instant Replays

Great profit coaches never rest on their laurels.

Your profit attitude determines your profit altitude.

"Departmentalism" destroys teamwork and will destroy your chances for winning the Profit Game.

"Always praise a player in front of his peers. Never criticize him in public."

— Larry Pecattiello, Coach, Detroit Lions

Great coaches are never afraid to admit they've made a mistake.

PEP focuses everyone on the profits needed to grow the company and add value to it.

PEP provides the support and monitoring of progress that effective implementation requires.

Players play harder when they know their work will be rewarded.

Often it's the shoemaker's kids who are the ones going without shoes.

PEP supports your company's strategic goals. It doesn't change them; it enhances them with the bottom line results of additional opportunities.

Great coaches learn from other winning teams.

Employees are your most valuable resource. Coach them into a winning Profit Team.

Organizational Structure—Is your staff organized to work effectively?

There is nothing more unprofitable than making unnecessary work more efficient.

Marketing & Sales—Are your sales people getting enough chances to run with the ball?

If you can't measure it, you can't track it and you can't manage it.

Sales feed egos, but profits feed families.

Cross-Sell—Sell all of your products all of the time. What are you providing for free that you can charge for?

Pricing—The customer is the driving force when it comes to selling prices.

Create a whole new profit culture where your Profit Team keeps scoring.

Develop your own play book with all your firm's successful strategies recorded and ready for winning the Profit Game now and in the future.

# Chapter 7

# THE END ZONE

The Profit Enhancement Process will change your thinking and change the profit*ability* of your entire business.

Stop now and think about this. Researchers tell us that the average person has more than 50,000 thoughts a day. That roughly amounts to about a thought a second. Day in and day out, each of our minds are endlessly engaged with thoughts…we call it "thinking."

Without question, any positive mental activity is good and the more the better. This time, let's look more closely at this 50,000-thoughts-a-day statistic as it applies to each and every employee at your company. Maybe now their thoughts are like this:

> "I really don't think there is anything more we could do to increase profits. We're doing everything we can, I'm sure."
>
> "It's not my responsibility. That's not my job."
>
> "I wonder what I'm supposed to be doing here."
>
> "If they'd ask me, I could show them a thing or two about how to run this place."

But, what if their thoughts were like this:

> "I've got an idea!"
>
> "I can't wait to show the Profit Activities Leader this idea."
>
> "Wow! They liked my idea and ran with it."
>
> "I'm the one who made the difference."

The essence of creativity and engaging life to the fullest is our ability to ponder as many new thoughts as possible. You are the team leader, it's up to you to make it happen with ALL of your team.

Too many of us find ourselves thinking today along the same lines as yesterday and the day before, just doing it "*the way we've always done it.*" All too frequently, we continue mulling over the same stale ideas and beliefs, re-inventing the wheel, and even dwelling on the same problems and worries. By dwelling on the same thoughts over and over again we limit our capacity for unique, creative thoughts—no matter how simple.

---

Unrealized profit opportunities exist in every business.

---

Revenue-generating ideas that are discussed, but never implemented, as well as other ideas never even brought to light, hide numerous opportunities for bottom line profit.

The mission of the Profit Enhancement Process is to get you to leave behind old, stale thoughts and open your mind to undetected, rewarding opportunities and new profit*ability*. This profit*able* thinking can come from you, of course; but equally as important, it will come from every one of your employees who lives and breathes and grows and thinks in the profit-enhanced profit culture developed within your company and embraced by you.

This new profit culture is the first big step in order to make your business completely profit*able*. Change the way you and every employee (your Profit Enhancement Officers) think. Establish a new culture that raises your awareness of the world of opportunities around you and *see* profit*able* ideas, opportunities and activities at every turn.

And that, in a nutshell, is the foundation for the concepts

behind the Profit Enhancement Process you've just read about in this book. With it you succeed at profit*ability*. Without it you are far more likely to stumble over the profit fumbles. It's that simple.

Thinking and the thoughts you and your Profit Enhancement Officers choose to occupy your consciousness, will control your company's future. These thoughts, shaped by your Profit Plan, are the most powerful forces shaping the course of your business. These thoughts, shaped by your Profit Plan, in fact, are the most powerful forces your company's minds will ever engage in.

Thinking and the expression of thought have shaped your company from its birth to the present. Unquestionably, you are where you are and what you are because of the thoughts that have dominated your mind and the minds of your employees. As for the future, your destiny is being shaped by thought and the Profit Plan you will lay out to steer those thoughts, right at this very moment. Thoughts dominate our lives. Thinking thoughts in accordance with "The Plan," however, drives your company's team to winning plays.

To be of value, this challenging concept must be learned and relearned over and over again. It's the kind of idea that must become the culture of your business. And it can be elusive. Even though many acknowledge it, only the committed truly understand and grasp its meaning, leave behind the masses and play to win.

How can something so simple elude the vast majority of the business world? The answer to that question is really quite clear. Some people choose to control their company's destiny, engage their employees in the winning culture, and build lives of success, wealth, and happiness for their Profit Teams—while others don't. Some *choose* success, and some don't. It's as simple as that. The concepts of the Profit Enhancement Process are available to anyone who chooses to be coached in them and use them.

Your Profit Game Plan controls your company's life, profit and bliss. You can choose to make it work for you.

So, in conclusion, how important is it for your business to have a Profit Plan? It's vital. It's like the game plan for winning the Super Bowl. It's a plan that focuses all thoughts and all thinking of everyone in the business on the bottom line—no matter what their job is. It's the plan for realizing your true profit potential. Imagine what it will do for your company and your valued employees.

Take what you've learned about the Profit Enhancement Process and implement it in your business. All you have to do is decide and take action. Remind yourself often of the Latin adage *carpe diem*, which means, "Seize the Day!"

Take the initiative now to choose the Profit Enhancement Process. It's a system that delivers never-ending profits and real value to businesses that manage it effectively. It's your game plan for winning The Profit Game if everyone on your Profit Team knows how to play—and how to win!

It's a process that has generated hundreds of millions of dollars in recurring year-after-year profits for clients of members of the Institute of Profit Advisors!

If you are ready to take your business to a new level of profit*ability*, give us a call at 1-800-WE-PROFIT.

Or visit us on our website http://www.weprofit.com. Members of the Institute of Profit Advisors are trained to coach you on how to play and how to win The Profit Game—a game worth playing!